T0164686

# the
# PRAYER
## of
# LOVE

# *the*
# PRAYER
## *of*
# LOVE

DR. MARK HANBY
*and*
ROGER ROTH, SR.

**HOWARD BOOKS**
A DIVISION OF SIMON & SCHUSTER, INC.

New York   Nashville   London   Toronto   Sydney   New Delhi

Howard Books
A Division of Simon & Schuster, Inc.
1230 Avenue of the Americas
New York, NY 10020

Copyright © 2012 by Dr. Mark Hanby and Roger Roth, Sr.

First Howard Books hardcover edition September 2012

HOWARD and colophon are trademarks of Simon & Schuster, Inc.

For information about special discounts for bulk purchases, please contact Simon & Schuster Special Sales at 1-866-506-1949 or business@simonandschuster.com.

The Simon & Schuster Speakers Bureau can bring authors to your live event. For more information or to book an event, contact the Simon & Schuster Speakers Bureau at 1-866-248-3049 or visit our website at www.simonspeakers.com.

Designed by Jaime Putorti

Manufactured in the United States of America

10  9  8  7  6  5  4  3  2  1

Library of Congress Cataloging-in-Publication Data

Hanby, Mark.
    The prayer of love / Mark Hanby, Roger Roth, Sr.
        p. cm.
    1. Love—Religious aspects—Christianity. 2. Love—Biblical teaching. 3. Bible. N.T. Philippians I, 9–10—Criticism, interpretation, etc. I. Roth, Roger. II. Title.
    BV4639.H235 2012
    241'.4—dc23
                                                                    2012004794

ISBN 978-1-4516-6908-4
ISBN 978-1-4516-6909-1 (ebook)

This book is dedicated to my family—and especially to my parents, who have been my greatest teachers of love, acceptance, and forgiveness.

It is also dedicated to the thousands of individuals who have at some point and in some way shared the stage of life with me—some who have shown extreme love toward me, some who have had great displeasure with me, and some who have given me no thought or regard either way. You also have been my instructors.

I love you all!

*Mark*


For my wife, Karen. You have seen both the loving and the not-so-loving sides of my nature and have had the wisdom and grace to create an environment where we could walk together in the pursuit of love. May your great love be returned unto you manyfold.

For my sons, Joseph, Roger, Ryan, and Kevin. The desire of every parent is for their children to prosper and have a significant impact for good upon the world. I realize that you have all surpassed your father in many things, including ability, spirituality, and above all your willingness to love. This gives me much joy. Thank you.

*Roger*

*Now the glory of these three will remain with you forever, faith, hope and love, but the greatest of these is love, for love is the ultimate expression of your faith and hope. Love never fails!*

—AUTHORS' PARAPHRASE OF 1 CORINTHIANS 13:13

# CONTENTS

# ACKNOWLEDGMENTS

---

We would like to acknowledge two very amazing people who were instrumental in the publication of this book. The content of this book had been gestating in our minds for a number of years, and it was their loving care and wisdom that brought it to birth. Natasha Kern, our literary agent, has been the unique combination of advisor, advocate, consultant, and most notably friend. And Rebekah Nesbitt, editor-in-chief, Howard Books, provided indispensable input and direction that made this book a reality. Thank you both for your love and support.

---

To all who seek the transforming power of love, I would like to give a powerful and bold prayer that has been empowering people through the force of love for more than two thousand years. It is a simple fifty-nine-word prayer that has the power to unlock the marvel of love. Its words and thoughts have profoundly and thoroughly affected my relationship with God and with others. Thousands who have learned to make it part of their lives have been transformed through the peace and liberty it brings to those who dare to pray to live it.

You are in possession of life's greatest mystery—the desire for giving and the hope of receiving love. Love is a universal force. It cannot be restricted by age, gender, social class, political philosophy, ethnicity, financial status, or religion, for then it would not be love.

In this book Roger Roth and I have included numerous personal stories, written from a firsthand perspective, that have been significant in our growth and understanding of love. As you read through this material, I believe you will come to see all the events of your life in a new light. Situations that have brought you joy and especially those that have been accompanied with regret will take on new significance. The events of your life, especially the difficult and painful ones, will find resolution through the eyes of love.

I, like many of you, have suffered through dark moments in the pursuit of love. And like many of you, I have known the atmosphere of supreme joy that surrounds the giving of love and the immeasurable fulfillment that accompanies receiving love. I've come to realize that the gift of love is not usually a chance happening—falling upon us at unexpected times—but is most often the result of discovering, understanding, and applying love's many facets.

The amazing prayer that is discussed in this book has come down to us through the wisdom of the ages. The seven aspects of this prayer are given in a particular sequence and must be understood and applied in the order given for the promised effect. The simple steps, **if followed in order**, will do for you what they have done for countless others: cause you to acquire and grow in an incomparable and unstoppable love. Most of us have had neither a means of measuring the degree or growth of our love nor an orderly process to help us through many of love's stumbling blocks and to achieve the possibility of perfect love. This process is the focus of this book.

Though the content of *The Prayer of Love* may not necessarily be religious, it is definitely spiritual. That is, the book reveals a supernatural pathway to love that is not limited to any particular religion, culture, or socioeconomic standing. Prayer at its heart is not a ritual of words but is simply a thought lifted up and God's response to that thought. God's response is always one of love. Many have considered the possibility of perfect love to be only a concept, but I know that it can become a growing reality in anyone's life, as it is the ultimate hope for our struggling world.

Please join me in discovering this prayer and its power to activate a growing love in yourself and those around you.

I salute you for choosing love,

*Mark Hanby*

For inquiries, please contact info@theprayeroflove.com.

Mark Hanby's website is www.yourquantumlife.com.

# the
# PRAYER
## of
# LOVE

# INTRODUCTION

---

We are bleeding at the point of our most intimate
relationships!

—MARK HANBY

*I* am guilty. I openly confess that I have not always made
the most of my opportunities to love. In each of our lives,
we have known people who cause us nothing but frustration and pain. If we are honest, all of us at times have
done the same to others as well.

If we've been fortunate, however, then we have had a few
special people who have chosen to love us while looking past
our imperfections and blemishes. Life presents each of us
with daily possibilities to mature and grow in love, but most
of us do not recognize these opportunities because they often
come disguised as problems and disappointments. This is
where understanding and learning to pray "The Prayer of
Love" can bring about a love transformation in your life.

Love is an eternally important topic. It is the wellspring from which all life receives meaning. Love knows no geographic, ethnic, social, religious, or cultural boundaries. Whether people realize it or not, it is the central motivating force in their daily lives.

We live in a materially prosperous world the like of which has never been seen in the history of humankind. Even the poorest among us, because of modern technology, have a standard of living that surpasses that of kings and nobles from earlier centuries. If happiness were based upon material possessions, we would be the happiest, most well-adjusted generation ever to live on the planet, and yet the opposite, unfortunately, seems to be the case.

## We Are Bleeding from Our Intimate Parts

We are bleeding at the point of our most intimate relationships. For all our wealth, we have alarming rates of litigation, murder, suicide, divorce, drug abuse, and social unrest. Though we as a people desperately desire love, how to mature and grow in love remains elusive for many. I at one time was stuck exactly where so many are today— between a need and desire for true love with all people and an inability to make that desire a continuous daily reality.

I had known about "The Prayer of Love" for some time, but the catalyst for unlocking its power came during a conference at the New Orleans Superdome. On the platform with me were more than three hundred noted evangelical and charismatic leaders from across the nation. The expectant assembly that had gathered was eager to hear whatever we speakers had prepared.

As I stood before the seventy thousand enthusiastic attendees meeting in that arena, it suddenly dawned on me that what we on the platform and those in the audience needed and inwardly desired was something that could never be provided by the delivery of pithy messages in an auditorium setting.

The text of my message that evening was about the woman with the issue of blood who was healed when she touched the hem of Jesus' garment. As I spoke, it became increasingly apparent to me that the point of the message was not only for the hearers gathered that night but for a hurting world as well.

This woman had had a severe medical issue for twelve years. She bled from her female parts day after day without cessation. She was bent over and could not stand erect. She was bleeding and slowly dying from her most intimate parts.

Within my spirit I heard the words "People are slowly bleeding to death at the point of their most intimate relationships." Like this woman, foundations have been destroyed and roadblocks to loving relationships have been erected. What the attendees at that conference needed—indeed, what we all need—was a way to stop the bleeding. We are a society at risk, not because we lack material necessities, but because we do not know how to have meaningful, intimate, and loving relationships with those around us.

When in my mind's eye, I saw the woman touch the hem of Jesus' garment, I could see love flow through Jesus and stop the flow of blood in the woman as she became completely restored. The Apostle Paul's prayer of love instantly came to mind, and I once again sought out its secrets that would cause maturity and growth in love.

# THERE MUST BE MORE

Many of us today are similar to this woman. We cannot function properly because the pain and fears from bleeding relationships have left us bent over and unable to see properly. This woman had spent all she had on physicians, but instead of getting better, she only grew worse. We do the same thing—go to conferences, purchase the latest self-help materials, and follow the latest teaching fad only to find our desire for growing love and relationships further away than when we started.

Seeking love, we often find ourselves searching after a variety of self-help and life-transformation measures. At the heart of most of these efforts is a desire to find acceptance, meaning, and transformational love. We are crying out in our spirits, "Is this all there is?" There must be more. Like the lyric "looking for love in all the wrong places," every day we find others and even ourselves going to great lengths and engaging in often-misdirected efforts to try to stop the emotional bleeding in our lives.

Back in the late 1970s, I was invited by some eager searchers to accompany them to the final night of a week-long spiritual discovery seminar, "Discovering Inner Peace and Spiritual Power," that they had been attending. As the evening started, the entire group was whipped into excited displays of activity by divergent musical sounds and by the participants' loud chanting. After some time, the attendees, with eyes closed, were led into humming a single low note as the leader, in theatric fashion, uttered statements of approval for the gatherers to ponder. The crowning event of the seminar was to have the faithful demonstrate their newfound spirituality by walking in bare feet across a bed of hot coals.

The leader, in a show of faith, went first, followed, one by one, by those who had paid large sums of money in an attempt to discover spiritual peace and power. As each person scurried across the coals, they were met with cheers of approval and embraces from others who had crossed before them. For the most part, they left in a mood of elation hoping that the week had brought them a measure of the spirituality they had been seeking.

The event organizers used the last evening to encourage the invited guests to participate in an upcoming seminar and discover what the gathered faithful had experienced. Amid the excitement and after witnessing something they thought was a near miracle (coal walking), many enthusiastically signed up for the next session.

I did not sit in judgment of those gathered, but I did wonder at how willing these individuals were to seek out some measure of spirituality, to find some means to greater fulfillment and purpose.

About a week later, Emma, one of the persons who had invited me, stopped by my office. I asked her how things were going and if she and her friends were still feeling the inner contentment and elation they sought to demonstrate on that last evening of the seminar. In a disheartened tone, she said, "I went to the seminar because I had this longing that there must be more to life than what I was experiencing. After this fading momentary high, I am still saying to myself . . . there must be more."

I believe this feeling—that there must be more—is a universal human desire. It is the desire to find not only a meaningful and fulfilling life but also to discover that which secretly underlies all our desires: to locate the full dimension of love.

I was reading in *Time* magazine an article entitled "Change We Can (Almost) Believe In," and it reminded me of the story I just recounted. It is an article about the events inside the sweat lodge at the Angel Valley Retreat Center outside of Sedona, Arizona, where eighteen people were hospitalized and three died in their quest for spiritual discovery. James Arthur Ray, who conducted the retreat at Angel Valley, was charged with manslaughter and ultimately convicted on three counts of negligent homicide. But he is not a weird, on-the-fringe guru; he's in the mainstream of today's spiritual transformation movement, having been seen on *Oprah* and featured in the best-selling DVD *The Secret*.

The article describes how the $10.5 billion self-improvement business utilizes books, DVDs, courses, seminars, life coaching, retreats, infomercials, and various other devices to fill the human hunger for self-improvement and spirituality. So great is the desire that the top dozen motivational speakers each are able to average almost $25 million in yearly income.

At Angel Valley, fifty-five participants paid thousands of dollars for a week of what could be described as a form of compliant torture in order to learn to let their "higher self" guide them to feel "the power of the earth beneath them and the Angels above them."

Angel Valley shows us how far people are willing to go to find spiritual transformation. Though I believe such methods will never bring a lasting result, I do not fault those who go to such extremes to satisfy the crying of the human soul for contentment and meaning. Unfortunately the methods that most choose will never answer this sincere cry. I have learned, from "The Prayer of Love," that only spiritual maturity anchored by love and not self-reformation brings lasting spiritual transformation.

So we are encouraged by the modern self-help movement to reform our attitudes and actions in order to bring about contentment and spiritual transformation. Though this may be beneficial for many of us, the attainment of spirituality does not reside in human effort. Adjusting the way we think and act may increase our income or massage our ego, but alone it will never bring lasting transformation or the discovery of an unstoppable love.

Instead, the key factor in growing in love and spirituality is praying for and receiving spiritual maturity from God. It will change the way you act and think, though not as a consequence of human effort or following systematic self-help techniques, but rather as an almost effortless result of learning to allow growing love to freely enter and flow through your being.

Maturity, in the human sense, is the taking on of responsibility appropriate with age—acting your age. Most people have matured naturally to be able to read and work and become productive members of society. These same people may never have matured spiritually to live beyond anger, self-pity, frustration, anxiety, or adolescent attitudes and desires. As my father used to say to me, "Wearing a size eleven shoe does not make a man a man."

We have linked our world through the power of the Internet, but as yet we are unable to connect it by the wonder of love. For love to consume our world requires spiritual maturity—the capacity to receive, to give, and to grow in love, regardless of conditions, obstacles, or circumstances that would seek to limit it.

Though we speak of fulfillment and discovering our spirituality and purpose, underlying this is really a need to access a love that is able to activate these in our life. This often hidden desire, to go beyond life's limitations and discover an avenue to abundant, growing, and never-ending love, is at the heart of our efforts to bring about self-reformation and spirituality. *The Prayer of Love* is the understanding and the method to make this desire a constant reality in our lives. It is the answer to the yearning "Is this all there is—there must be more!"

# TEN YEARS TO LEARN ONE LESSON

I was raised by wonderful parents. My father was a minister in a very strict denomination, an organization with a myriad of rules and regulations for "proper Christian conduct." Although what constituted proper conduct varied somewhat from church to church, there were various rules on acceptable dress and social behaviors.

When I was twenty-three, I was invited to pastor a fledgling church in Fort Worth, Texas, which was part of this same denomination. Although I was well known, even at this early age, and had the ability to pastor a church, I admit that my lack of spiritual maturity in some areas was a hindrance to helping the church achieve spiritual growth and transformation.

The legalism produced by the required rules and regulations of conduct had caused people to superficially judge one another by what they did and how they looked rather than by who they were. These rules were rooted in fear and the result of trying to protect people from perceived negative worldly influences. Fear always causes people to judge others by external behavior, rather than through understanding a person's heart. This, of course, is a common condition of many in society, whether they are religious or not. This improper judgment was not unique to us alone, but, in our case, was manifested through our self-imposed rules of conduct where, in other places, this judgment may reveal itself in various other ways.

The rules we created and confused with the Word of God had taken the place of spiritual maturity. Spiritual maturity gives us the ability to see as God sees and to give up the security of our fears for the liberty found in love. Over time we as a church developed a great maturing love.

It takes maturity to change and to stand in the face of opposition. It takes courage to challenge your attitudes that may be rooted in improper judgment. The events that were unfolding caused many of my peers to disassociate themselves. It is a strange reality that fear of change causes some people to prefer the security of bondage to the liberty of spirit, but to those who obtain the maturity to change, there is great reward.

After pastoring for about a decade, I preached a sermon that had been developing within me for years entitled Brickyard Churches and Junkyard Dogs. I told the church, in a facetious manner, that they no longer needed God, because they had me to tell them what to do. I told them how to dress, when to come to church, how to pray, and to pay their tithes and I answered whatever need they had at the moment.

In my sermon I was describing how many churches were like brickyards patrolled by junkyard dogs. Their members were in a perpetual state of immaturity needing someone to constantly tell them what to do rather than having the maturity to walk in love. Instead of the liberty of a mobile energetic church that walked in the world in the maturity of the spirit, their prejudices allowed them to be a place where their fears of losing out on God and spirituality were translated into inappropriate attitudes, improper judgment, and a need for control.

We had a great revelation of the grace of God. We decided to stop doing everything God never told us to do and start focusing on love and its power to transform, not by effort but through maturity. We began implementing some of the principles found in Paul's prayer of love— though at the time I didn't recognize this prayer as the condensation of those principles—and it dramatically changed us. Rather than focusing on external behaviors, we began to focus on the heart. Instead of a self-righteousness attitude that demanded obedience to a law of do's and don'ts, we started to search out and discover the divine uniqueness of each individual. The maturity of grace did for us what legalism was totally incapable of doing.

It is at this time that we began to see a great change and growth in our congregation. Lives by the thousands were transformed, and we saw healings and miracles. As I look back on those days, I see that this did not come about because of any wisdom or power on our part, but because we dared to see what would happen if we opened ourselves to the rule of love. This was only a beginning, but it was a great beginning.

God's desire is to heal a bleeding world. Love is the only power that can deliver us from our bleeding issues and bring about true spiritual transformation. Emma's longing—"there must be more"—is our longing as well, and its answer is found in discovering and applying "The Prayer of Love." There is more, much more. Trust love above all else, and let it and not your own efforts transform you by the majesty of its power.

# 1

## FUNNELING LOVE

*When love and maturity work together,*
*expect a masterpiece!*

—ROGER ROTH

Written on the pages of the book you are now holding is an astounding little prayer able to dramatically change your life. Its words do not merely offer knowledge, but more importantly are expressions of truths that have the ability to bring complete and lasting spiritual transformation.

Many people today will never reach their full potential or become the person they sense is hidden inside. They long for purpose, meaning, and fulfillment—to live a life of love—but have difficulty in finding it.

I know how they feel. In fact I have ministered in conventions and seminars on six continents to thousands who have felt just that way. Good people who desire to grow in love beyond their frustrations and weaknesses.

Through much adversity and by the help of God, this is what I've found. For all my struggle and disappointment, the answers to life's most difficult situations are usually simple. In fact, God is a God of simplicity.

We make life difficult. We complicate life and we complicate the simplicity found in God. Nowhere is this simplicity more evident than in this statement: "God is love"!

*This prayer has the power to give you a lifestyle of love!*

Jesus summed up the secret to life in one very uncomplicated yet profound statement—that we should love God with all our heart, soul, mind, and strength, and love our neighbor as ourselves. To do this is the fulfillment of all of God's requirements.

God is love. That is His essence. To find love is to find God. To live a life rooted in love is to fulfill His commandments. Our ultimate purpose is to discover, to express, and to be ruled by love.

## LIFE EXPERIENCES ARE INSTRUCTIONS ON LOVE

It is important to see that everything that has happened in your life has provided for you an opportunity to mature and grow in love. This is especially true of people and events that have caused you disappointment, struggle, or loss.

What others may perceive as your failures are really opportunities to develop spiritual maturity. If you can learn to embrace life in all of its joys and sorrows, you will find that through these, God is continually providing instruction for discovering and growing in love.

We often have trouble being real with one another, especially those of us who consider ourselves to be people of faith. To be open and truthful about our doubts or struggles puts us in a very vulnerable position. People are often eager to criticize or condemn us, but far less willing to accept us despite our failures or to love us in our human frailty.

I don't want to burst anyone's bubble, but there are no spiritual supermen or superwomen even among religious leaders. There are those, however, who have learned how to take the worst attacks that life has to offer and turn them into glorious victories by learning to love.

We all too often demand perfection from those around us while conveniently overlooking our own shortcomings. Yet most every Bible figure who was used greatly by God overcame significant imperfections. Moses exhibited fear and disobedience, King David was a murderer and an adulterer, and even the Apostle Paul was a blasphemer and persecutor. Nothing you've done, and nothing you are, is worse than what they displayed, yet God loved them and used them in spite of their failures. So instead of running from your weaknesses, use them as opportunities to change and as instructions for growing in love.

When I was a young boy, our family lived on a small farm in Enterprise, Ohio. The schoolhouse and general store were about a mile down the road and I would often walk this road on the way to school or when my mother would send me to get some groceries. On my way I would pass by farm fields and three or four houses.

In one of these houses lived an elderly couple in their seventies. I always dreaded walking by their property for they usually saw me and made it clear in no uncertain terms that they did not like me. They were always angry and very provoked when I would pass by. They would holler things like "Get out of here, boy; we don't want you near our property" and "What gives you the right to bother us? You look like you want to cause trouble!" or "If you come on our property, you're going to get a whippin'!"

A train track followed the road on the back side of the houses. To escape these people, sometimes I'd walk the track instead of the road, but it seemed more often than not they would spot me, and let me have it with their unkind comments. When we lack maturity, it makes us want to run away from difficult situations, and I certainly wanted to run away from this one.

I remember coming home from school one day with tears in my eyes from a particularly hard tongue-lashing at the hands of these cantankerous people and asking my mother, "Mama, how come they don't like me?" She said, "Honey, something very painful must have happened to them, and you remind them of it. Those are the kind of people you need to love." My mother was not only very wise; she was spiritually mature. Some parents would have perhaps belittled these people, or become angry and lashed back at them, but my mother just held me and calmed me and taught me how to love the seemingly unlovable.

> *Divine blessings are a gift of love. When we bless others by our words and actions, we give them the same gift.*

One Saturday in late autumn, my mother sent me to the general store to get her some baking supplies. While at the store, I overheard someone talking to the store clerk about this old man who had taken very sick and was confined to his bed. On the way home, I saw the elderly woman trying to chop wood. When I got home, I told my mother what had happened, and her response made me very uncomfortable. When we choose to love in difficult situations, it often makes us uncomfortable. My mother said, "Mark, I want you to put your coat on and go over to their house and cut their wood. No matter what they say to you, I want you to cut and pile their wood. They heat their house with wood and need your help." I thought, Oh great, I wish I had kept my mouth shut!

When I got to the neighbor's yard, I stepped as softly as I could toward the woodpile. As soon as I started chopping the wood, the woman came out and yelled, "What do you think you're doing, put that ax down and get out of here!" I said, "Sorry, ma'am, but my mama said I was to chop this wood and not to come home until it's done, no matter what you said." She stood on the porch and watched me for most of the afternoon as I chopped and split and piled that firewood on her porch.

When I was done I said, "When you get more wood, let me know and I'll chop and stack it for you." She grabbed me and hugged me for a long while as she wept over me. She said, "I had a little boy once. We lost him when he was just about your age. Maybe he would have been like you."

After that, they would always wave to me as I passed by or call to me to come over to the porch where they would have a cookie or some treat waiting for me. I spent many hours in their house as they talked with me about all kinds of things. We became very good friends, and when we had to move to another town, I missed them greatly.

We are eager to judge people's behavior, but very slow to discover their heart. I think it should be the opposite. These people for decades had grieved over their only son and did not know how to deal with his loss. Their behavior showed them to be bitter and resentful people, but that was not who they really were; that was only their attempt to deal with their pain. My mother's maturity and a willingness to love set these people free.

# MADE PERFECT IN
# OUR WEAKNESS

---

$P$raying "The Prayer of Love" has radically changed my life. Its lessons took me most of a lifetime to learn. When I decided to write this book, I committed to be as genuine as possible so that others might discover this powerful pathway to love.

I've been in formal ministry for more than fifty years. When I was a young boy, my parents would have me memorize whole sections of the Bible so that by the time I was in high school, I had memorized large portions of scripture. When I was seventeen, I started to preach in places across the country, with amazing signs of the Holy Spirit.

In the 1970s, when I took over a church in Fort Worth, Texas, I was still in my twenties. That church grew to become one of the first megachurches in the nation. I was considered the "golden boy" of my denomination and started ministering throughout the world.

In South Korea I spoke to more than five hundred thousand people in one day, and God did marvelous and mighty things in our midst. In India the mass of people was so great that when I called for those who needed healing to come to the platform, they had to pass the sick overhead from hand to hand as they were delivered from all sorts of diseases and sicknesses.

I remember when we first built our new church facility in 1972, it sat 2,500 people—and with the balconies and overflow, it would seat 3,500. We were only a few hundred people at the time, and the place seemed empty. We were wondering how we would ever fill it. It was at this time that I spoke the message described in the introduction, Brickyard Churches and Junkyard Dogs. This is when we first started to apply some of the aspects of "The Prayer of Love." One day I heard in my spirit the words "I will do notable miracles," and I believe it all centered around our humble beginnings and a desire to walk in love.

One Sunday I felt compelled to pray for a blind visitor to our church who worked at the courthouse. His milky eyes had been totally blind for years. I said, "Clem, do you believe you can be healed?" He was honest and said, "I don't know." I thought, Oh boy, what's going to happen now? So I said to him, "If Jesus were here, do you believe He could heal you?" He said, "I think He would." In response

*Spiritual maturity comes when we are willing to learn life's lessons through difficult circumstances.*

I conveyed to him that, "Jesus is here and He wants to heal you." When I said that, he began to reach out with his hand as though he were trying to find where Jesus was. Instantly I could see the milky substance run out of his eyes as his sight was completely restored.

Since he was well known and greatly respected in the community, the news of this miracle spread abroad very quickly. The next Sunday the church was so packed, there were people standing in the aisles and out the doors trying to get into the building. God continued to do many numerous and notable miracles as the church continued to thrive. This was not due to our efforts, but in response to seeking His love.

I've had the privilege of giving more than 3,800 sermons that have been recorded in various forms. Along with noted and prominent ministers from around the world, I've ministered at countless conventions and seminars to thousands of people. Hundreds of thousands of my books, as well as ministry tapes and CDs, have been distributed worldwide.

I mention the above blessings not to elevate myself or my ministry, but to make a very important point about maturing and growing in love. As great as these events may be, they pale in comparison to what I've learned and received from His love. The truth is that all the above were the result of God's grace and action, and not because of any ability or spirituality we possessed.

Though God has blessed and given me a great gift, He has taught me that the blessing and gift are of Him and not of my own efforts or abilities. My desire to grow in love was ultimately birthed far more from God's discipline to develop spiritual maturity than from His blessings.

I know what it is to be rejected and to be cast aside as having no value and to lose material comforts, to have people I never would have believed could turn against me make the most vile and hurtful comments about me through no fault of my own. I've witnessed friends and dear people isolate themselves from me, and have wept for many days as a result.

I also know what it is to suffer because of my own indiscretions. I've experienced my life shaken to its roots. Spiritual maturity has taught me that much of the pain I've experienced has been due to my own failures and that I could redeem those sorrows through love.

In all these things I've learned far more about receiving and giving love from my seasons of struggle than I ever did from my times of blessing. By praying "The Prayer of Love," God has unleashed the great power of love so that like the Apostle Paul, I count all things as of little value compared to acquiring His love.

At one of the lowest points in my life, I discovered this prayer, and it radically altered my perspective and brought a continual atmosphere of love's presence. It's wonderful to live in a continual place of peace and love, and it is available for everyone.

I want you to know that you are not alone. Whether you have found a wonderful measure of love and just want to learn how to receive more, or if you feel love has eluded you and you don't know where to turn, the prayer of love will change your life. Love is not meant to be an occasional experience, but a daily excursion where peace and joy rule in your life continually. The desire to understand life by embracing love will change your perception. Your ability to continually embrace and grow in love is as close as your willingness to understand and pray this short yet powerful prayer.

What benefit did I receive from following my mother's instruction to help this neighbor? I was no longer afraid to walk by their house. They became very good friends to me, and I learned that love is the most powerful force in the universe. When we choose to love, everyone wins.

# A SIMPLE PRAYER WITH UNLIMITED POWER

It is a short seven-part prayer spoken by the Apostle Paul but it contains the secrets for being transformed by love. It was a prayer he spoke over people whom he loved deeply and without reservation to ensure that their love would continue and grow.

Before we examine this prayer, let me explain the circumstances that led to its being prayed.

After Paul's initial enlightenment, he experienced years of training, rejection, and imprisonment. He would come to devote his life to bringing an understanding of truth, purpose, and destiny to many along the shores of the eastern Mediterranean. The first place in Europe that he taught was in the city of Philippi (in what is now Greece), around 49 AD. It was here that he and his companion were severely beaten and thrown into prison, and it was here that, over the years, he would develop a very special bond of love for those in the city who followed his teachings.

This Jewish apostle to the Gentiles, by his own account, lived a life of much deprivation and rejection. He was beaten, abused, left for dead, often hungry, falsely accused, and in peril continually. Yet the love he found was greater than the material comforts he sacrificed.

While in a Roman prison with his ultimate sacrifice drawing near, Paul wanted to perhaps one last time send encouragement to those he so loved. In a cramped, dark, damp, rodent-infested, stench-ridden cell, as his own death was looming, he determined to send words of life to the Philippians. He ate his food, shared with the surrounding bugs and rats, from a carved-out bowl in the cell floor. As he pushed his own waste to a small hole in the center of the cell, his heart was not full of regret and anger at his condition, but teeming with love for God and others.

In circumstances that would have most of us crying "God, get us out of here!" Paul was at peace; his heart was full of love. How is this possible? What secret did this Apostle discover that has escaped the rest of us?

Love so transformed Paul that he was totally free of what men thought of him or what they could do to him. He would now pray this same transforming power over the Philippians.

From prison near the end of his life, he would write instructions to the followers at Philippi. Included in his instructions was a prayer providing a lasting guide on acquiring, developing, and maintaining spiritual maturity that would ensure their continual love. In his love he was seeking divine guidance for those who were so close to his heart. Thinking he might never see them again, he decided to write them a letter.

He loved them. Their memory was always before Paul. He watched out for them as a father for his children, wanting to make sure that the work begun in them would remain even after his death. Paul's prayer for them was made with joy, calling them partakers of "my grace."

In what was possibly his last contact with them, he most certainly wanted to give parting words that would help them overcome—words that would show them how to continue on their path of love toward fulfillment and destiny. These words formed Paul's prayer for them.

*And this I pray, (1) that your love may abound yet more and more (2) in knowledge and (3) in all judgment; (4) That ye may approve things that are excellent; (5) that ye may be sincere and (6) without offense till the day of Christ; (7) Being filled with the fruits of righteousness, which are by Jesus Christ, unto the glory and praise of God.*

This was not just a short fifty-nine-word prayer, but also a pattern for the Philippians to follow in growing and maintaining spiritual maturity. The seven parts to this prayer—love, knowledge, judgment, excellence, sincerity, harboring no offense, and walking in righteousness—form a pattern for developing, measuring, and growing in love.

Paul knew that for the Philippians to complete their spiritual walk all the way to their destiny required a pattern easy to understand and follow—a pattern that would show them exactly where they were on their spiritual journey. They needed a guide that would ease frustration and enable them to make adjustments so that they could steadily grow in love and maturity.

*The fifty-nine words of this short prayer form a pattern for us to grow in love.*

The seven points to Paul's pattern are spiritual benchmarks, not only for the Philippians but also for all who seek to grow in love and spiritual maturity. These benchmarks can be likened to a funnel, wide at the top and narrow at the bottom.

## All the Marbles

When I was a young boy, I engaged in marble-shooting contests. It was quite a fad. We would hurry to school to play before class, as well as fill our lunch hours, seeing who was the most skilled at playing "for all the marbles." All of the boys participated, as well as some teachers and a few girls. It was great fun, especially since I had become the champion marble-shooter in my little corner of the world.

Over a short period of time, I had won enough marbles to fill numerous grocery bags. When my mother found out what I'd been doing, she was not amused. She was against wagering in any form and equated marble-shooting with gambling.

When she saw the bags full of marbles, she said, "Mark, I want you to give those marbles back to whomever you took them from." I told her that it would be impossible, since there was no way that I could possibly remember which ones I won and from whom I had won them! She agreed to allow me to keep them, but made me promise never to play for keeps again.

If you know anything about marbles, you realize that they come in a great number of sizes, colors, and markings. The most common sizes ranged from half an inch to just over an inch in diameter. Some were solid steel, others were pure glass in a variety of colors, while others, called cat's-eyes, had interesting textured bands embedded inside so that they resembled the glistening eye of a cat.

We had, at that time, the old-style, large, glass milk

jugs with the tall narrow necks. My father had suggested that I place the marbles in them since the containers would be more durable than paper bags, and I would be able to gaze at them through the clear sides of the jugs.

You can imagine what happened when I took the grocery bags that were almost half my size and tried to pour the contents into a glass jar whose opening was only about an inch and a half. There were marbles everywhere! For every one I managed to get through the opening, three or four scattered on the ground.

*A tractor funnel from my boyhood became a gift from God for finding love. Every event in your life has significance.*

Witnessing my plight, my father got a large machinery funnel and placed it over the jugs' openings. I watched in amazement as the marbles were sorted effortlessly through the narrow orifice into the wide reservoir of those large glass vessels without spilling even one marble. In my later life this was to provide for me a powerful illustration of the process of acquiring love and spiritual maturity. The funnel had the ability to guide each marble without my effort or frustration.

## FUNNELING LOVE

Paul's prayer is like this funnel, able to order our life to produce love. We do not have to be in competition with one another. We do not need to experience continual frustration in our relationships. We are not in a race against others to attain notoriety, position, material prosperity, or spiritual enlightenment. In fact, if we understood the divine method for spiritual advancement, we would realize that we provide for one another's stability, order, and connection.

Being so "wide at the top," no one has to fear that they might not find the way. Being a funnel makes maturing in love almost effortless because the weight of love and the pull of maturity by themselves are sufficient to bring anyone through the pattern.

Paul's prayer is a prayer for maturing and growing in love that provides us with a spiritual funnel that, when prayed with understanding, without effort or frustration, will bring the divine power of love to rule and grow in our lives.

In the following chapters, I will offer you an understanding of the various aspects of this prayer that will, I hope, increase its power in your life. Make it a point to pray this prayer to yourself as your understanding increases. As you do, you will find God transforming you almost effortlessly by the power of love as you travel through this spiritual funnel.

Pray the following prayer each morning and evening until its words become ingrained in your mind and spirit. When that happens, the power of this prayer will bring forth the transformation of love. At the end of each chapter, it will be altered to reflect the teaching of that chapter. *A Study in the Prayer of Love* and *The Prayer of Love Devotional* are also available for your daily use.

## "THE PRAYER OF LOVE"

*And this I pray,* that your love may abound yet more and more in knowledge and in all judgment; That ye may approve things that are excellent; that ye may be sincere and without offense till the day of Christ; Being filled with the fruits of righteousness, which are by Jesus Christ, unto the glory and praise of God.

## POINT OF LOVE

.....................................................

*Open arms are a universal gesture of love.*

*They put the giver in a vulnerable position while at the same time offering the recipient total acceptance.*

*Be willing to take chances—love's reward is always far greater than its cost.*

# 2

---

## BOUND BY LOVE

*That Your Love May Abound
More and More!*

Life starts with love. Love is the power to change, to grow, to discover your destiny, and to manifest the image of God inside of you.

At the widest part of our spiritual funnel is the first part of "The Prayer of Love"—that your love may abound continually. It is a prayer to find and grow in a love that is ever maturing. It is a vehicle to understand how to allow love to totally transform you and deliver you from all your fears and self-imposed limitations.

Abounding love is love without boundaries. Your fears,

frustrations, prejudices, and pain are all boundaries to growing in love. Through understanding gained from praying this prayer, you will begin to become inoculated from these self-limitations.

Day by day, you will acquire an unstoppable ability to develop and grow in love. As you make your way through the spiritual funnel of "The Prayer of Love," you will find yourself acquiring a spiritual maturity that will bring greater order, strength, and grace into your life.

Since love is an infinite subject, it is impossible to ever fully define or totally grasp all of its characteristics. We can, however, become lifelong students of love and continually develop an understanding and expression of love in our lives.

## Benchmarks for Gaining Maturity

The seven parts to Paul's prayer form benchmarks for acquiring and growing in love. When we talk about benchmarks, we are referring to a means of measuring maturity. In many ways these benchmarks are measurements of our ability to give, receive, and grow in love. Love is the moving force of the universe. It is the force that causes all people to live rightly and to respond properly in every situation.

Its presence gives us courage, faith, and a resolve to connect with our divine purpose and destiny. Its absence turns us inward and isolates us from one another. Ultimately love is the cry from God to us and from us to God to return to our created purpose.

So when we talk about abounding love, we are talking about the God kind of love. Think of being in a place where your confidence, your peace, your self-worth, and your willingness to love cannot be affected by the attitudes of others or the circumstances of life. A place where you are not restricted by evil, but where the maturity of your love continually reveals God to a world desperately in need of Him.

This kind of love is a love without conditions. It is a love that allows you to love your neighbor in the same degree that you love yourself. We need love without boundaries; in other words, we put no boundary or limitation on our willingness to accept people.

This does not mean we accept everything they do or turn a deaf ear to evil. It does, however, mean that we do not allow their occupation, their social status, their ancestry, their sexual orientation, or their disagreeable attitude to be conditions for withholding love from them.

Stephen showed such love in chapter eight of the Book of Acts when he was branded a heretic and stoned to death. Those who had nothing but evil to say concerning him, he loved. They reviled him, cursed him, falsely accused him, and stoned him, yet in all his physical pain and torment, his last words were to forgive those who were about to put him to death.

*You are continually judging yourself by your attitudes and actions toward others.*

If someone says something even a little hurtful to many of us, we may become upset for days. We may even build emotional fences to keep that person at a distance.

I once knew a man who would not speak to his mother, father, sisters, or brothers. For twenty-six years, until his death, he would not attend family functions, nor did he even go to his parents' funerals. This all because he felt snubbed at a family gathering.

None of us have likely gone to this extreme, but who among us has not kept certain people at a distance for fear of being hurt? Could we, in all honesty, say that we could demonstrate the love that Stephen showed under similar circumstances?

Yet God has given us the same ability. Most of us may tolerate our enemies, but very few have learned to love them. "The Prayer of Love" can mature us to the point that we can even love our enemies!

What effect Stephen's love and maturity had on the Apostle Paul, when Paul was a chief persecutor and agreed to put Stephen to death, is not known in detail. It is interesting that after this event, the Apostle Paul had his conversion.

Undoubtedly Stephen's love for his accusers, including Paul, demonstrated a godly love that Paul, in all his religious upbringing, had not experienced. Abounding love is not an acceptance of evil or the wrong actions on the part of another, but rather it is an openheartedness toward everyone and a refusal to hate and reject another. You may not agree with the lifestyle or actions of someone, but you realize that every person, even those who may be seriously depraved, possess human dignity because their life originated in God.

# Love Without Conditions

Few people have learned to love unconditionally. In conditional love, our love for another is conditioned upon their response and attitude toward us. We judge their worth by how they make us feel. People we fear or those who are disagreeable, we love less than those who bring acceptance and encouragement.

When we have conditional love, we are always trying to decide whom we are willing to love, and whom we are willing to overlook as not being worthy of our attention. We pick and choose among people who meet our conditions as being acceptable to love.

My response in loving is conditioned upon my attitudes, preconceptions, and prejudices. This is why the use of labeling of individuals and groups to build boundaries is contrary to love.

People are unique, and they are individuals. Even though they may share some common traits with others—as to financial status, ethnicity, education, religion, physical size, and the like—attempts to identify individuals solely according to labels place predetermined conditions on a willingness to love.

You are continually judging yourself by your attitudes and actions toward others. This is what Jesus meant when he said, "Judge not lest you be judged," for with the same measure that you judge is how you will be judged.

This is one reason why the first benchmark of "The Prayer of Love" is so powerful. When you pray "let my love abound," you are tearing down self-imposed walls—you allow yourself access to be loved and to love others as well.

When you pray "let my love abound," you tear down fences you've built, which limit God's love from reaching you. "Let my love abound" is a prayer of liberation and carries with it the potential of divine power and love.

Love is that huge, open-ended willingness to make ourselves available to everybody. We don't usually approach most people with open arms and open minds.

In life we have a tendency to build walls and fences. We do not even like some people, because we never open our hearts to find out who they really are. Or our first opinion of them often poisons our hearts, so we are never able to see beyond the surface.

Abounding love is love that grows. If love grows, then it is not the same at the beginning as it may be later on. If that is the case, then it has to be tinted with and have hues and shades of growth.

Love is like the rising of the sun. On a dark night, you see the beginning of the light in the eastern sky and know dawn is coming. You welcome the dawn. Although it is not light yet where you are, you know it is coming. When love dawns on us, it has the potential for growth if we don't limit it with conditions.

Most of us have been in the woods when it is totally dark, and then in the faint reaches of the forest have seen the eastern sky starting to lighten. In a short while and at times almost in an instant, the light reaches up and the trees start throwing a shadow. Once you can see shadows, then you are made aware that life is moving. If love abounds, then it has to grow. You can see the illumination of love as the dawn turning into morning.

*"Let my love abound" is a prayer of liberation and a prayer of power.*

Sometimes even without knowing specifics about a person, you become willing for the light to approach you. The light gives you a greater clarity about who they are and what they are, and how you should respond.

After a while the sun gets up so high, you can see a dewdrop on a stem of grass as it turns in the wind. When the sun pilgrimages over that eastern horizon, it turns every dewdrop into a diamond, but when you walk to where there is still darkness, it only makes your feet wet. So, love is an anticipation of allowing light (what is true, as opposed to what you might assume is true) to clarify the position you are in as it relates to other people.

When we start talking about the outer fringes of love, that is where we really get tested. Most of us can love those who love us, but what about those who don't appreciate us, or those who look on us without kindness?

## LOVING THOSE WHO DON'T LOVE YOU

"The Prayer of Love" is your opportunity to love even your enemies.

How can you love your enemies?

By definition they mean no good toward you, they desire only to bring you harm. They have rejected you, and the danger is that, in rejecting them rather than loving them, you may become like them.

Though loving all people does not mean that you position yourself to be repeatedly walked over, you need to maintain an open heart toward everyone. If you close your heart, you add another row to your defensive wall trying to protect yourself from pain and hurt. In so doing, you not only limit your ability to give love to others but also hinder your ability to receive love from others. What you have to do is to keep your heart open so that you are relating to all people, or even to an enemy, through a desire for love.

You need to be able to see through the eyes of love, instead of through predetermined judgments. In doing this, you allow time for the sun to rise on that relationship, so that you become willing to walk in the light of forgiveness. You become willing to offer the light of repentance and willing to offer the light of acceptance to discard the darkness of offense. As the light grows brighter, your love is wide enough that you can actually accept someone who, at one point, was an enemy.

You may not have the ability at this moment to say you love everybody, regardless of what they have done to you. You may not be able to love all others in the same way you love your child, but if you keep your heart open, love will enter and abound. There are hues and shades and levels of love. I've found that the fact that I can grow in love means that my love at present can be greater than it was in the past.

I can say I love to fish or to hike but these are things I

enjoy and things that make me comfortable. I don't really love them; what I do is like and appreciate them. I can only truly love that which has life.

Love is not all one sided. To have love, there must be a giver of love and a receiver of love. When you drive by a military cemetery with the little white stones crisscrossed in every direction, you can see them by the hundreds gleaming in the sun. These are final markers for men and women who lost their lives in past wars. Most of us get emotional at such sights.

Do I love the grass or the headstones, or do I love what they remind me of, or do I love the bones that are under glistening markers? Do I love the fact that at one time they were alive, at one time they served, at one time they gave their lives? What I really love is the love that was in them that made them willing to die for something greater than themselves. In giving of themselves to protect and benefit others, they became in many ways the manifestation of God.

Love has desire, love has appreciation, and love has loyalty. It has many aspects. Truly, love is a many-splendored thing. The hues and tints of love are all the emotions that surround it.

Now if love abounds, it is possible that my love can

become a rainbow that has all of these colors in it. That would be what we would call unconditional love. Unconditional love is not conditioned by my desire, not conditioned by my needs or conditioned by other things; I really love regardless. Love covers great faults and failures.

I love beyond my emotion. I begin to understand that if divine love had conditions, I could never have changed. It is this fact, that divine love is unconditional, that allows me to change and grow.

Love had to overlook my faults and weaknesses, or I could not have grown. I would never be able to know or express the multicolored facets of love.

Love may be like a quilt or like a Navajo tapestry: in order to see the picture or in order to see the pattern, all the yarn cannot be one color. You need dark ones, and then you have midtones, and then you have perhaps red and bright blues and yellows, and you have browns and some amber and some deep violets, and all of these are emotions that surround love.

Abounding love is when you are willing to take the individual emotions and attitudes, good and bad, and situations, pleasant or troublesome, and allow them, regardless of their nature, to increase your love. When you are willing to open your heart, then you can take all of the

good and the bad, and say you are willing to have the maturity these produce
"woven into the fiber."

How I feel about my country, my
loved ones, my desires, my personal feelings, those who are unfriendly toward
me—all of those things are fibers in a
great tapestry called love. Spiritual maturity allows me to stand back and look

*The hues and tints
of love are
all the emotions
that surround
abounding love.*

not just at the dark strings, but at the entire picture.

So my view of the world is that I love my enemies, I
love my neighbor, I love my friends, my wife, my children.
Obviously the love of God is a different kind of love, but
love of God has to be added to human love in order for us
to ever be able to say that we are willing to embrace the
whole picture.

When you pray "let my love abound," you position
yourself to receive understanding on what it means to
abound—no boundaries, no fences, ever growing.

It is an attitude that is willing, in its openness, to
accept things beyond your personal opinion, beyond your
personal preference, and beyond your fleshly desires. Your
love has to become unselfish because opinion, preference,
and desires are all selfish emotions.

That is why you need to love others as yourself. Your preferences, desires, position, determination—all these things that color your own life and who you are, need to be the vantage point from which you view others. It is the golden rule. To truly love your neighbor, you have to be willing to respect his or her opinions, preferences, desires, and dignity.

## BECOMING INCLUSIVE INSTEAD OF EXCLUSIVE

So loving your neighbor is not so much an emotion that just makes you want to grab your sweaty neighbor over in his yard and hug him real good, and say, "Oh brother, I really love you!" I don't think that is what love is really all about.

Love is accepting the fact that he mows his yard at one thirty in the morning and, instead of standing by the fence and shaking your fist at him, you say, Well, there may be some reason that he could not do it at four in the afternoon.

Love makes you willing to seek information and make allowances about another's conduct, so you can see things from his or her perspective. Perhaps he is a nut for mowing his lawn at one thirty in the morning, or perhaps (as has happened) he is suffering from senility and could use your help, rather than your ridicule.

So love saves me anger, it saves me disgust, it saves me many things. Love presupposes opinion. You notice that some people draw opinions very quickly on who people are and what they are like.

Poorly developed opinions often hinder us from seeking to find the good in a person, and they are usually formed out of our fears or prejudices. If a person does something we don't like, we may be very quick to form an opinion: Why do they do that? Or, why don't they do that? Or, that is so stupid! Why would anyone be out mowing their yard at this time? Only an idiot would do that. They are rude, noisy, disturbing people, and there are babies who want to sleep. You have all of these opinions, but love would presuppose that.

Before you draw those opinions, make all those comments, say all those things that really change your attitude toward that man, you need to see from his perspective. You are thinking there's got to be some reason why he is doing that, reasons that he understands and you don't.

Now sometime I may talk to him and ask him why. I

may suggest that he do it at some other time, but I am not going to presuppose that this man is an idiot. If I saw things through his eyes, is it possible I would change my opinion? If I knew all the facts, it may be that I would be more apt to respond in love and understanding than to harshly accuse him.

## A TRUE STORY OF MISTAKEN INTENTIONS

It is like the true story that happened in a Dallas law firm one Thanksgiving. The head of the law firm always gave out a large turkey to his associates for the holiday. A group of attorneys from the office thought it would be great fun to play a practical joke on the newest member of the firm, a young, single lawyer who had recently graduated from law school.

They took one of the turkeys out of its wrapping, removed everything, and stuffed that wrapping with paper and weights so that it perfectly resembled a real turkey. The only part of the bird that remained was the neck that protruded through the small opening at the end.

They all chuckled with delight as they thought of him opening the turkey and finding only a neck. They could all envision his response, and it brought laughter every time they thought about it.

At the end of the day, the senior partner gathered all the attorneys in the boardroom. He gave them each a turkey and wished them happy Thanksgiving. As was arranged, they saw to it that the young attorney got the sham turkey.

That night the young attorney proceeded as usual with bird in hand onto a bus for a thirty-minute ride home. At one of the stops, a mother with two young children sat down on the seat next to him. It was apparent that they were not affluent.

He thought, What am I going to do with this turkey? It's way too much for me and obviously she could use it far more. He wanted to give it to her, but he said to himself, no, I don't want to embarrass her, so I'll tell her that I got it as an office gift and if she would like it, I would be happy to sell it to her for two dollars. The woman excitedly agreed, and the young attorney went home feeling he had done a good thing for someone less fortunate.

The next Monday when he returned to work, all the other attorneys were anxious to see his response. When he did not respond as expected, they asked him what had happened. Upon hearing the unfortunate outcome of their little practical joke gone awry, they explained what they had done and thought to make it right with the woman who purchased the turkey.

That night and for the rest of the week, all the attorneys rode the buses in that area hoping to find the young woman and explain what had happened. They never did find her. Can you imagine what this woman's opinion of that attorney might have been after opening up the package and finding only paper and weights?

It would have been very easy for her to form the wrong opinion.

We often form opinions that would have changed if we'd had a fuller understanding. This is why, no matter how hard it may be to figure out someone's actions, we need to choose to love and to give the benefit of the doubt to others.

Love is the perfect representation of proper attitude. What I do, how I react, what I say, how I am willing to endure over the long run becomes the manifestation of the divine in the world.

Love will always make me hope for the best and give others the benefit of the doubt. Love never desires to wrongfully acquire what others have, because love cannot come to us by taking, but only by a process of giving and receiving.

*To truly love your neighbor you have to be willing to respect his or her opinions, preferences, desires, and dignity.*

As I grow in spiritual maturity, I don't react like other people react. I don't do what other people do. I don't say what other people say, and I don't judge their value by the way they speak and act.

I don't do that because I have a set of benchmarks that allow me to grow in love and to understand who I am. My worth does not come from whom I know or what I do for employment or because of my natural looks or abilities.

## INSTRUMENTS OF LOVE

Love comes through a variety of avenues. When love is received, the one receiving it becomes a mirror of the one who gave it. This is why true love between people is endless and can grow. This reflection of love is not limited only to people.

Humans are the highest reflection of God's love, but not the only reflection. When we receive the love of God, we become like Him, and in doing this, He is revealed not only to ourselves but also to others. All of God's creation is a reflection of His love.

Many people have a pet or an animal to which they truly give great affection. Unlike our love of country or a job or a homestead, love of animals is different because animals are not only recipients of love but can also be givers of affection. They teach us an aspect of God's love for humankind and for His creation. Animals are part of the world that God created for man to oversee. The world itself is a reflection of God, and animal life, next to human life, is perhaps the highest representation of that love.

That a special bond can exist between humans and animals is evident to most. Recently, there was the story of a cat, for example, that had the ability to know instinctively which residents of a senior care facility were going to die even when this was not evident to the medical staff. And there are many stories of animals who have fought to death for their owners. This kind of loyalty goes beyond mere training and instinct.

I've seen many examples of the special bond between

humans and animals and believe it can, indeed, be a manifestation of God's love on the earth.

Recently, I was speaking at a church in Wisconsin that is praying "The Prayer of Love" and studying its principles. One aspect of "The Prayer of Love" is learning to receive God's love. If we perceive from God's point of view, then we realize that a perpetual cycle of love is manifested when someone gives loves and someone receives love, and the one that receives love gives love in return.

This church was focusing on the fourth stage of "The Prayer of Love," asking God to increase the parishioners' love in discernment. As a church, they began praying a simple four-word prayer—"Amaze Us, Oh God!" As they prayed this prayer daily, they gained a renewed awareness of God in every aspect of His creation. People were spared from serious accidents, marriage and family relationships were healed, and financial needs were amazingly provided for. Most important, they began to see themselves as extensions of God's love, and the power of love flowed throughout their city.

The Sunday after I spoke, a woman attended the service and heard testimonies about seeing things from God's perspective. As she thought about the various ways God speaks and cares for us, she said, "God is going to amaze me today." Before she fell asleep that evening, she prayed, "Amaze Us, Oh God!" Her husband had been on a weekend camping trip with some friends and was not expected home until late.

She was awakened in the middle of the night and could hear their dog making a commotion downstairs. As she approached the living room, she found the dog trying to wake her husband. He had fallen into a near–diabetic coma; with great difficulty, she was able to revive him. She said, "God saved my husband through our dog. I was not only amazed by that, but by the fact that the avenues of God's love are almost limitless if we are willing and able to see them." God uses all creation to reveal His glory, and if our eyes are open, we can see, rather than a world of turmoil, that the world is really a reflection of God's love in many ways.

## My Worth Does Not Come from Other People

Your worth comes because you know who you are in God, and how you are connected to the Spirit of God. If your opinions and your feelings are not shaped by love, then you will have a harsh demeanor toward others. Since God is love, it allows you to love.

Unfortunately many think it is God's desire to punish and inflict pain on those who fail to agree with Him. This is because their attitude about God is shaped by their own opinions and fears. They don't really understand that they are loved by God, so they don't know how to love others without condition. If spiritual maturity is a manifestation of a spiritual lifestyle, then how you react to people, how you accept people, what you think and what you do, have to be framed by some force in you.

If that force is love, then you are going to respond from the Spirit, and if you don't have love, then you will react out of your carnal nature. This is why how you love yourself—and how you love others—becomes a barometer of your spiritual maturity.

The opposite of love is not hate; it is fear—specifically, fear of being rejected or of not being accepted by God and other people. A fear of rejection is the source of all our fears. If we understand and have experienced that we are accepted by God, and He will never reject us, that His love is eternal and constant, then no other fear can rule in us. A fear of loss or a fear of death or a fear of heights or a fear of poverty—all are rooted in a fear that deprives us of the security of love. Perfect love casts out all fear. Not love, but perfect love casts out all fear. Love doesn't just compensate for fear or help us with our fear; it casts out fear.

In this world there are so many walls built by so many people. Even within families, there are walls between parents and children, and in society, walls between teachers and students, and between employers and employees—these are all walls built to protect egos, but also walls that can isolate.

These barriers all tend to bring forth this terrible thing that happens in our world called dysfunction. People cannot function, and the reason they cannot function properly is usually because of terrible insecurity and the fear of not being accepted. Insecurity—not being secure—is also a result of fear. I am afraid of what my neighbor will think, I am afraid of what people say, afraid of how my kids will cope with life, afraid of my boss. I am afraid. I am really afraid that they are not going to respond properly, or not do what I think they should do.

*Love is the perfect representation of proper attitude.*

People who have put up roadblocks to love are literally ruled by fear. Rather than kindness, these roadblocks often represent themselves in gruffness or meanness. Anger, malice, strife, wrath, envy—these are works of our carnal nature and the result of fear. Love, however, will produce fruit that comes from the spirit and is revealed as joy, peace, long-suffering, gentleness, kindness, and meekness.

This is why those with abounding love have a different attitude. Someone who understands they are truly loved by God has a different attitude.

It is an attitude that people long for; it is an attitude that people want; it is an attitude that is magnetic; and, it is an attitude that really should be drawing people to seek out their divine connection. We have learned to love systematically or selectively.

I love you if you love me. I'll love, if it doesn't cost me too much. Do I want that "if"? Love that is selective always has an "if" in it. It still is love if it has that "if" in it, but it is conditional love. Conditional love is "iffy" love. Abounding love always gives. It causes us to lay down our life—that is, to lay down those things that limit our ability to love or accept others.

Love lays down its life. Love gives, fear withholds. Love surrenders, fear threatens. If somebody truly loves, then they are willing not just to give things, but willing to give themselves. Conditional love is willing to pay money to do things for people, but unconditional love makes us willing to give ourselves. Real love manifests by giving what money can't buy.

Our carnal nature, in its simplest form, is disobedience or an opposition to the love of God. So it is anything that opposes love. My lifestyle will either be shaped by love or by my fears. Abounding love is a growth process.

## All Things Work by Love

When you pray with understanding "let my love abound," you set in motion spiritual forces that cannot be held back. It has to abound and get bigger until it becomes unconditional. All things work by love. All things. Nothing will work if it is not first of all framed in a willingness to change our opinions and attitudes. Instead of taking, I am giving. Instead of wanting, I'm sharing.

Love requires a change, from my carnal mind that is shaped in fear, to a desire to connect to God shaped in love. This is a real lifestyle change that will start manifesting in how I treat my wife, my husband, my children, my employer, people I hardly know, and those whom I have a hard time knowing. It will change how I face situations and how I deal with problems.

Love is a harmony rather than a dissonance. It seeks accord rather than discord. Love understands that no matter how we classify ourselves or others, love overcomes everything and is the appropriate response in every situation.

Love supersedes all and has an open opinion not based on preconceived ideas. Love is greater than evil. Love is willingness to understand and to show mercy to those who may have injured us. Love seeks harmony. Love seeks to harmonize. The truth is that love is a universe; *uni-verse*—one verse, one song of harmony, and that harmony is really the love of God. We learn to sing the same song. It is the opposite of discord.

If a boy and a girl fall in love, they have things that they say they have in common, common feelings. The thing that tears them apart at some point is discord. One is playing one song, the other is playing a different song—both are trying to play their different songs at the same time. Love is playing the same song and singing the same song.

Love changes our spirit. It brings peace and joy where there was confusion and hopelessness. The benchmarks of "The Prayer of Love" are really a hope for human deliverance.

Benchmarks are a roadmap for deliverance from a carnal nature to the divine nature. They are a pathway, a clearly marked pathway of seven benchmarks that gives you hope of getting out of this terrible maze of a frustrated life into a place of harmony, acceptance, and rest. And it all starts and ends in love.

Abounding love is being able to love beyond circumstances, to love beyond what would normally turn into disappointment. It allows you to love beyond your anger and to submit your rights to the test of love.

I have a right to feel that way. I feel infringed upon, and that's what cancels my love. Without abounding love, we will always feel we have the right to revert back to an old nature. In order to have abounding love, we need to understand that it has to be a love that is willing to grow. Most human love is something that we like, and we add an extra embellishment to it and call it love.

Love is the enduring principle that underlies all human life because love is God. As discussed earlier, God is love, and if God is in our life, we can eventually even love our enemies.

Love becomes such a foundational principle to us that

we understand love is given by God, and the people on this planet are God's children. They may not as yet have realized their relationship to God but God nevertheless loves them. Therefore, we have an innate ability to respond as God responds to us: in love.

*People who put up roadblocks to love are literally ruled by fear, but love rules in peace.*

Only in having God's nature am I able to respond to them as God responds to them. I cannot be part of the redemptive process leading to the time when all people will be reconciled to God, if I do not have the mind of God and the perspective of God toward all people.

Love is a necessary component of maturity, because if I do not see life situations and people through that redemptive maturity, then I will revert to that same carnal alteration that made them like they are. I become like they are. They are angry with me, so I get angry toward them. They revile me, so I revile them; they curse me, so I curse them back.

If I love at the same response level at which they love, I fall to their level of lack of redemption and immaturity, and I can never lift anybody.

# Finding a Higher Place

I have to get into a higher place, a transcendent place of love in order to become part of the God process that loves so much that it is able to draw others toward God. Learning to pray "let my love abound" is the first step in seeing as God sees.

Abounding love has two parts: One is that love is a foundational virtue that can grow (it is a growth process like plants that start out in seed and end in fruit). The second part is that I start perceiving the world differently than I have perceived it before so that my love can grow. If I don't realize that my love can grow, then I just say, "Okay, I'm not going to hate them anymore. I'm going to try to love them." But that doesn't actually change anything. I might change my language but I really don't change my mind.

*Conditional love is love but it is "iffy" love.*

Love can only be activated by love from without. God first loved us. He gave us the power to come out of our carnal nature back into fellowship with Him. As long as I try to alter the human process of love to try to become a better person by self-reformation, I never grow and I never mature. Though self-reformation can be beneficial, it can never be complete. I alter my attitude only as much as I am humanly capable. So when someone cusses me out, I say I'm not going to cuss him back. I'm just going to say, I love you—but down in my heart, I still have this anger and a wrong attitude.

So love becomes a basic spiritual attitude. I have to realize that love must really have a response system to grow, and then if it grows, it does not just change how I talk and how I act; it changes how I view others and the world, through the eyes of God.

Before it can do this, it has to change how I view myself. God is love. If I see myself as having divine connection and being made in God's image, then I can love as He loves. I can bless those who curse me. In order to get to that point, I cannot just change my mind; I have to get a God perspective. It is very necessary for me to understand that my love has been stunted and needs to grow. When it gets the right spiritual soil and fertilizer, it starts to grow, but it is a process, just as a child grows from youth to adulthood. It is a growth process that brings forth spiritual maturity.

# A ROADMAP FOR LOVE

The key to love or God's love in us is recognizing God in everything and everyone. Without it, we are totally incapable of loving unconditionally. So if someone murders your child, how is it possible that you could love that person? That kind of love is almost incomprehensible. Yet God loves all people, even scoundrels, villains, and murderers. He does not love their evil actions, but He does love them. Yet if we are honest, it is extremely rare to find an individual who can see past evil and love all people.

Instead, you love the love that's there—the God that's there, because Jesus died for that man. Jesus' love and forgiveness are available to every person, even the worst among us. What we would normally do is withhold God's love from the worst. With just my human ability to love, my natural ability, I cannot love someone who has taken something that is precious from me or has done evil to me or others.

The benchmarks of the Apostle Paul's prayer of love are our roadmap toward that end. Only love can separate us from our fears, frustrations, prejudices, limitations, and pain. The distinction is not that I accept or overlook evil or a person's wrong actions. It is not that we don't judge or punish wrong actions and maliciousness on the part of others, but rather that we are able to see beyond the present circumstance and see what God sees.

This kind of love comes only by spiritual maturity. It is the kind of love that while judging the sin, still loves the sinner. If I have abounding love, then my love goes beyond anyone's actions, deeds, demeanor, or attitude. It goes to the fact that if God loves them, then my ultimate expression of love would be to love them as well.

God doesn't love their sin, God doesn't love murder, God doesn't love rape, God doesn't love any of those things, but He loves the individual. So I love what He loves, and I disapprove of what He disapproves of.

We can look at God's love like this. Someone has a child who is perverse and rebellious. You can be disappointed, you can be angry, you can be hurt. You can exercise tough love, for example, by leaving a child in jail when you could have posted bail and had him released.

Deep down, beyond all that, while not overlooking wrong actions, you love an individual because you can see

*Love is the enduring principle that underlies all human life because love is the substance of God.*

what God sees in him. Your close relationship with someone has given you the ability to see what God sees.

It is in learning to truly hate sin, but not the sinner, that unconditional love becomes a reality. This, however, cannot happen without the development of spiritual maturity in our lives. The seven benchmarks are aids for understanding and praying "The Prayer of Love." At the end of each chapter, the prayer will be adjusted to emphasize the particular area discussed in that chapter.

## "THE PRAYER OF LOVE" FOCUSING ON ABOUNDING LOVE

*And this I pray, <u>that your love may abound</u> yet more and more in knowledge and in all judgment; That ye may approve things that are excellent; that ye may be sincere and without offense till the day of Christ; Being filled with the fruits of righteousness, which are by Jesus Christ, unto the glory and praise of God.*

## POINT OF LOVE

*All things work by love!*

*Love is not a feeling or an emotion;*
*love is the underlying force of life.*

*At the heart of the scientist's quest for a*
*"theory of all things" they will find that love is the*
*energy that allows the universe to exist.*

# 3

---

## SPIRITUAL KNOWLEDGE
## IS SPIRITUAL POWER

*That Your Love May Grow in Knowledge*

(The mind) in itself can make a Heaven Hell,
and Hell of Heaven.

—JOHN MILTON

---

The second benchmark of "The Prayer of Love" is knowledge—that your love may grow in knowledge. Today, there has been an escalating effort to acquire and utilize knowledge. We are living in the information revolution premised upon the adage "knowledge is power." I see many who feel that if they only had access to the appropriate knowledge, their lives, in every area, would become prosperous and well adjusted. Human knowledge by itself is not and cannot be the answer.

Our society has focused on education as the ultimate means for solving its ills. The feeling among many educators, civic leaders, and counselors is that knowledge of the damaging effects of drugs, racism, broken marriages, depression, sexual promiscuity, gangs, and the like will somehow greatly reduce or even eliminate these harmful behaviors and attitudes.

Yet the evidence does not bear this out.

Knowledge by itself can never bring change to struggles that lie deep within the human spirit—instead, these changes come by love through spiritual maturity. Learning to pray "let my love abound" in all knowledge opens the process of divine knowledge that is able to bring a spiritual alteration by allowing love to grow beyond human limitation. For love to grow, we need a knowledge that helps us understand and walk in Christ. This knowledge will reveal our spiritual identity, purpose, and destination. This knowledge will be rooted in a spiritual perception of God and our connection to Him. This kind of knowledge is the vehicle that allows love to be the answer.

Once you make love your ultimate goal, spiritual maturity will bring you to the place where you no longer have to focus on ridding yourself of negative thoughts and actions. This is the place where you start learning what God knows. This is the place where you acquire, as your possession, the knowledge of God and not merely knowledge about God.

At this place you not only learn about spirituality, but you become spiritually aware and begin to walk supernaturally. This is a knowledge found only in God. This is the knowledge that Adam and Eve gave up in exchange for the knowledge of good and evil.

## FRIENDSHIP FOR HIRE

I was watching an ABC News report recently on an Internet business popping up in cities across the world; people looking for friendship can go to this site and hire a friend by the hour. Most of these sites are legitimate businesses and offer purely platonic relationships. People rent companionship so they can have someone with whom they can dine or go to a movie or just talk. Typically the fee is $10 to $50 an hour, plus the cost for such things as food or theater tickets.

Now I'm sure there are some good, commonsense reasons why someone would utilize this service, but it does illustrate just how isolated we as a society have become. We have cities with millions of people, yet within those cities are lonely, abandoned people who have great difficulty in maintaining even marginal relationships. For all of its benefits, technology has given us a throwaway culture and, unfortunately, a throwaway attitude about people. People are far too often viewed as problems rather than treasures.

A friend of mine who makes his living by selling the latest in communication devices was lamenting to me that, in his opinion, our ability to stay connected with people has never been so great, and yet people have never been so isolated. We have e-mail and voicemail, iPhones and iPads, Facebook and Twitter, yet less and less personal communication. My friend said that his fellow workers would rather text him than speak to him. Face-to-face verbal communication for many is at an all-time low and waning every day.

When we have to pay for friendship, we have suffered great loss as a culture. For all our technical knowledge, our communication is mostly superficial. We need a spiritual technology that can once again help us to communicate heart-to-heart and not just device-to-device.

# LEARNING WHAT GOD KNOWS ABOUT YOU

---

The knowledge spoken of in the Apostle Paul's prayer is a knowledge of God. This knowledge is the opposite of the knowledge of good and evil. The knowledge of good and evil had to be present to give humankind the ability to choose between a carnal or spiritual nature.

As you pray "let my love abound in knowledge," God will begin to use the knowledge you already possess about a number of things to bring forth spiritual knowledge. As you seek to know Him, He converts your natural knowledge into spiritual knowledge. Everything we see is in positives and negatives. Everything is in opposition to something else to give us choice. The Bible tells us that God created the light and the darkness, and God created good and evil.

A culture that pursues knowledge about the natural world (natural or human knowledge) separate from a knowledge of God will advance technologically, but regress spiritually. The knowledge most seek is anchored in a quest to attain what is commonly called happiness by controlling their personal world and by acquiring material possessions. But true happiness lies beyond the material world and can only be found in manifesting spiritual maturity. What we need to be seeking is not just knowledge, but the kind of knowledge that will allow love to grow.

This is not natural knowledge, but a divine knowledge.

As humans we have all kinds of ideas about who or what God is, or if, indeed, there even is a God. Often we as people tend to make God in our own image, that is, according to our own perception. We then expect or even demand that others live according to that image. When our image of God does not live up to our expectation, we often get upset with God, yet He didn't let us down. Instead, it is our false image of who we think He is and how He acts that has let us down. All too often we have acquired a knowledge about God but not a knowledge of God. For love to grow, we need the latter.

It is in acquiring this knowledge that we discover our potential to love. This knowledge begins with learning that we are made in the image of the divine with the ability to change, grow, and love. Our life has purpose and destiny, and we have the ability to transform from natural to spiritual lifestyles.

The accumulation of human knowledge and the corresponding explosion in technology are rapidly changing our world. To many, this is a great source of insecurity; to some, it is a wellspring of opportunity. Never in the history of the world has access to the collected knowledge of humankind been so abundant. This information is no longer housed solely in universities and libraries, but made available to all via the electronic transportation and the information highways. The Internet brings to our fingertips almost limitless information. Without a degree, without ever having gone to school, even eight-year-old children have become proficient on computers. If access to knowledge were the answer to acquiring happiness, then we of this generation ought to be the happiest people of all time. Yet this generation has an epidemic of teenage pregnancy, suicide, and drug and alcohol consumption.

Human knowledge is insufficient when addressing the hopelessness and barren yearning caused by people who seek material abundance at the expense of spiritual prosperity. In a time when the material and technological advancement of society has never been so great, people by the millions long for meaning and fulfillment. We ask ourselves, how can this be?

As a society we are puzzled that there is such a poverty of the human spirit in the midst of unprecedented material affluence. This is because human knowledge in and of itself is not an answer.

Bookstore shelves are overflowing with "how to" and "self-help" books promising lasting change and contentment in ten easy steps. Websites are teeming with information promising better health, wealth, prosperity, inner peace, and satisfaction. Seminars and classes are available pledging to address every concern of life, and yet never has the earth's human population been more discontented, disconnected, and despairing.

*Knowledge is indispensable, but without divine influence, it is totally impotent in producing positive and desirable change.*

Knowledge is indispensable, but without divine influence, it is totally impotent in producing positive and desirable change. Knowledge without an understanding and practice of love may produce great material prosperity, but is wholly incapable of producing life transformation.

The growth of our love is dependent on acquiring knowledge. This is not a factual knowledge about figures, dates, and events, but a knowledge of who we are spiritually, what we are to be doing on the earth, and how to find true love that is found only in God. Thus for human knowledge to bring true enlightenment and spiritual change requires the influence and filter of spiritual knowledge.

When you pray "let my love abound in all knowledge," you are activating a spiritual force that will lead you to your divine image and destiny. You access divine knowledge of who you are and what is unique about you in the eyes of God. In discovering this, you will begin to understand why you act as you do, and you will acquire an ability to bring forth personal transformation. This awareness will help you understand that you are not a cosmic accident but a divine happening.

## THINKING BEYOND THE MATERIAL WORLD

We have been conditioned by society to think of life in material terms. Most view a lack of happiness to be the result of a lack of opportunity or a lack of money, but it is a lack of love and, more specifically, a lack of knowledge and maturity about love that underlies the general lack of happiness. People often confuse what they know with who they are. Knowing things does not make a person the expression of the things they know.

Human knowledge by itself causes us to believe that apart from spiritual maturity, we can find peace and happiness. Knowledge must be tempered with understanding and by practicing love, or it will never bring lasting change to the human spirit.

All true knowledge begins with a desire to seek and submit to God. The fear of the Lord is the beginning of knowledge. This God force is the repository of all material knowledge as well as spiritual knowledge, and it is infinite.

Generally, people are seeking to become happy by trying to control their material world. Even remote societies in the inner parts of China, India, and Africa are experiencing this illusion of trying to obtain contentment through material means. Western societies as well as most of the entire world have entered into a consumer age where people attempt to meet their needs, not by spiritual satisfaction, but by material gratification. The twenty-first-century man often thinks his lack of happiness equals a lack of finances, when in truth a lack of happiness is due to a lack of knowledge and implementation of divine love.

Many approach love as if it were a mysterious occurrence in our lives over which our attitudes and preparation have no influence. They often feel it can be experienced but not known.

We use terms like "head over heels in love," "finding love," "falling in and out of love" as though we are hapless recipients of its powers. Many who approach love as though it were the consequence of fate, never find it because they fail to understand that love comes through maturity as well as desire.

To pray "let my love abound" in all knowledge allows you to entertain thoughts about what love is, why it exists, how it can be acquired, and in what manner it can be passed on. This needs to become a practical activity on your part. We can only impart what we are. We can only testify to that which we have experienced. We can only give that which we possess. We can only understand that which we have allowed to change us.

We will resist what brings fear, but we will become what we behold. If we see and understand God's manifestation of love, we will become like it.

Only in knowledge of the divine and of our spiritual nature do we possess the potential to bring forth unconditional love. Through this knowledge will come divine favor, producing in us perfect contentment as it becomes multiplied in the knowledge of God.

Children cry to obtain love. In lieu of love, youth often succumbs to the conformity of peer pressure and an irreverent disregard for societal standards. As they age, people often fail to grow in love because they lack knowledge. They have no preparation, no maturity, no teacher, and no pattern. They fail to realize that love can be learned and grow, and this learning requires divine knowledge.

## BEING ALONE IN A WORLD OF LOVE

The word "alone" is a contraction of all one. So when we are alone, we seek to find within ourselves alone that which can only come to us through a higher connection and a love of others. Since peace, purpose, joy, and contentment are divine characteristics, they can come to us only through godly attachment. But love by its very nature requires focus on another for the object of its affection.

Our loneliness or aloneness is often due to a fear of not being accepted. We settle for living in isolation within ourselves, secure in not being rejected rather than engaging in the "risky" business of love. We all know what it is like to be rejected and to be found as unworthy of another's time, attention, or appreciation. The fear of rejection, with all the anguish and hurt that are associated with it, has numbed and isolated many.

When we reach out in love, we are most vulnerable. We put ourselves in a position where we are inviting others to place a judgment upon our worth. If they don't like what we say or if they do not accept us, it can cause us great mental and emotional distress. The pain and torment of a fear of rejection is the opposite face of love. And so many people choose to be alone, to control their situation, to keep themselves from distress by keeping the risk of judgment and failure at a distance.

So the way that you get rid of the hate, fear, and evil is through love. People are free to be who they are, free to choose life or death, love or fear.

You cannot force others or yourself to receive divine enlightenment. Intimidation, coercion, manipulation, and guilt are rooted in fear and can never produce love.

Religions, at times, try to pressure a response toward or acceptance of God by such tactics. These tactics, spawned in fear, war against a God awareness because all fear is a contradiction of love.

To hate or force our beliefs upon others is proof we do not know God. God is love and it is impossible to love God if we do not love others. We must learn how to discover love in ourselves and in others. The result of all true knowledge should be a progressive change into the divine nature. If knowledge does not change us into maturing toward this nature, then it is nothing more than empty human knowledge.

*You cannot force others or yourself to receive divine enlightenment. It comes through faith in peace, not through pleading or intimidation.*

We are all met with life forces and natural conditions over which we have no control, and we have two choices when it comes to this: we can turn inward by following our human nature in doing what would be to our benefit, make us most secure, and offer the least possibility for discomfort, or we can seek to manifest Christ who always manifests himself in love.

We have little control over many of the circumstances of life, but we have total control over our response toward them. We need to comprehend and empower Christ living in us.

## WHOM ARE YOU FEEDING?

When instructing me on choices and attitudes, my father used the illustration of two dogs with very different natures. As he would tell it, there were two dogs, one with a pleasant nature, and the other with an extremely aggressive and angry disposition. Their owner would leash them on separate chains so that only the last three or four feet of their restraints crossed each other. Being territorial by nature, they would often fight over this "no-man's-land."

Then he would ask me, "Mark, which of these dogs do you think won most often in its struggle for this common area?" I said, "I suppose the one with the aggressive and angry disposition, right?" He said, "Only sometimes. You see it depended on which one the owner fed the most." If we choose to learn and practice love, and to feed our divinity, then our lives will be ruled in peace with godly power; if not, they will be governed by fear and frustration.

To be totally immersed in life is to seek God in all things and to be willing to love under all conditions. Love creates; it never destroys. Therefore, creative activity is a manifestation of love. Attitudes that hinder this activity are hindrances to love.

I have no value.

I'm just an idiot.

The whole world is evil.

You can't trust anyone.

Change is bad.

People will only hurt you.

Do unto others before they do it to you.

All of these are attitudes that hinder creative activity. These negative perceptions give witness to the fact that we do not know how to love ourselves, nor do we understand the destructive forces that war against us.

Our perception dictates our response. If you perceive the world as being only evil or believe that God is angry with you, your response to other people will reflect that—you will find them lacking or you, too, will be angry with them. But if we see our own unique God likeness and see our distinctive value and purpose, then we will understand that God has unconditional love toward others and we will be able to manifest that same love toward them.

If we fail to see our own unique God likeness and do not see our distinctive value and purpose, then we will be incapable of manifesting an unconditional love toward others. We can only impart that which we are.

When we start to pray "let my love abound in all knowledge," you will begin to think about the way you think. Do you ever ask yourself questions about why you think a certain way? Do you ever ask yourself, "What motivated me to say that or to act in that way?" This is a great avenue for acquiring spiritual knowledge.

Spiteful and cruel comments and actions that bring emotional or physical harm will, over time, reinforce in us a belief that we are inadequate and lack value. When our perception of others is skewed, it continues to distort our view of ourselves and of God.

If we don't see ourselves as God sees us, we may feel that we are not good enough, that we lack value or that our existence is of little consequence or significance. If we do not recognize our godlike nature, we will yield to the lies that desire to cover up our true identity and imprison us in fear.

Unfortunately, the walls we've built to protect ourselves from pain all too often become a self-imposed prison. All fear is rooted in a lack of love. Some people are afraid of failure, afraid of people, afraid of anything that would strip off the mask and reveal the underlying insecurity and hurt. "The Prayer of Love" can become your vehicle to go beyond your fear and choose love.

## Seeing the Spiritual World

The spiritual world is completely the opposite of the material world. To those who are spiritual, the way to get love is to give love. The way to greatness is to become a servant. The more you give, the more comes back to you.

Unlike giving in the material world, when you give love, it is impossible not to have more than you gave. You cannot decrease. Just as giving knowledge increases understanding and giving honor increases authority, so giving love increases your spiritual well-being and reveals more of God to you.

Praying this second benchmark, "let my love abound in all knowledge," will help set you free from insecurity. To realize that you are unique in God and that no one can take what God has given to you brings great security.

Your godlike qualities are indispensable. When we learn to truly love our divine uniqueness, we acquire power over every other force that may come against us.

To those who are spiritual, the end of our life pursuit is the finding and giving of self, rather than material acquisition. In giving of ourselves, we unlock the power of love to others.

*Making your ear attentive to skillful and godly*
*Wisdom and inclining and directing your heart and*
*mind to understanding [applying all your powers to*
*the quest for it] . . . For the Lord gives skillful and*
*godly Wisdom; from His mouth come knowledge and*
*understanding.*

——*Proverbs 2:2,6 (The Amplified Bible)*

To seek and submit to the divine is the beginning of this knowledge. The foolish hate divine knowledge because they do not have the spiritual maturity to understand how their opinions and actions limit their ability to walk in the supernatural. God is not far away from any of us, and so our calling to Him always accesses a divine response.

## The Healing Power
## of Spiritual Knowledge

One of the nine gifts or manifestations of the Holy Spirit spoken of by the Apostle Paul is the manifestation of knowledge. This manifestation is an aspect of spiritual knowledge. Most people, whether they realize it or not, operate on some level of divine knowledge.

When I was at Fort Worth, a man from the congregation came up to me and asked me to pray for him. As I did, I had a revelation about him and his wife that I shared with him. I told him things in detail that did not come from human knowledge but supernaturally. Each of us has what I call spiritual circuit breakers that protect us in our communication with others. Discretion, weighing consequences, and spiritual prompting are some of these circuit breakers. Spiritual circuit breakers are the process where we allow all natural knowledge to be filtered spiritually.

In regard to me, my father described the process this way. He said, "Mark, let your brain turn over before you put your mouth in gear." Well, this man's wife did not let her "brain turn over." She began telling people, "Don't talk to Pastor Hanby, he tells everyone what you tell him." She thought that someone must have told me the things that I told her husband and, therefore, assumed I was telling everyone else. She became furious, rebuked me, and even accused her husband of telling me "secret" things.

I asked her if she ever considered that God knows all things and nothing is secret from Him. After speaking with me, she realized that the things I spoke about to her husband were not told to me, but came supernaturally. God used this to love and heal her. What she was so fearful of had put her into an emotional prison.

When she perceived that God really does know everything about us, it brought freedom to her. She understood that the things she feared were hindering her from receiving the answers her heart desired. Her relationship with her husband was restored, and she saw the power of spiritual knowledge as an attribute of God's love. We do not have to fear what God knows about us, but rather His knowledge possesses our freedom.

## Our Answer Is in His Knowledge

If we are immature, we cry and complain, and seek to run from life's unfairness and misfortune. Our immaturity causes our life experience to become a roller-coaster ride where we are happy when things "go well" and are discouraged and disheartened when things "go wrong."

We seek to be in control, but we are really out of control because non-godly attitudes dictate our response and sense of happiness. And so we strive to change life's circumstances through acquiring human knowledge but are never able to come to a knowledge of the truth. The only truth that frees and liberates is God's truth, found in Christ and available to all. Great knowledge comes when we stop cursing our problems and faults, and start to see that they are gateways into the divine.

I knew a man who had worked a certain job for eighteen years. He fully intended to retire in that job, until one day his plant went on strike and he eventually lost his position. He was not particularly happy with his job, but because the pay and benefits were good, he never sought to look elsewhere. When he lost his job, he became very angry. For months on end, he would complain about the lack of fairness and how he had been so wrongfully treated.

Several years later I met him, and he was very happy in a different job. As we talked, he told me that the loss of his earlier job had made him very bitter. Over time he realized that, though he felt wronged by his previous company, down deep he had really felt that God let him down.

At one point he remembered this "Prayer of Love" and started to apply it. He said when he earnestly asked God to let his own love abound in all knowledge, he began to see things about God and himself that he had never known.

It liberated him.

He told me, "Though this episode led to a fulfilling and prosperous position, what I appreciate most is that God used this to bring great love to me and my family. What I thought was a curse really turned out to be a blessing from Him, and all I had to do was desire to love. When I was angry about losing my job, all I could do was criticize and judge. My rotten attitude stopped the possibility of love, and everyone around me wanted to stay as far away from me as possible. When God intervened and caused me to seek His knowledge, I gained not only understanding but a greater appreciation for His love and care for me. I stopped worrying and resumed loving."

The Scriptures say that the rain falls on the just and the unjust alike, but because the mature seek the divine rather than cast blame and bemoan their misfortune, in the same circumstances as an immature person, they find fulfillment and wholeness because of their connection to divine knowledge. When we choose to live in love, we become renewed in knowledge after the image of God rather than after the false image of ourselves that we've manufactured out of our fears.

## DIVINE WHISPERINGS

Divine whisperings are continually spoken to each of us if we are sensitive to listen. They come to us in a still and quiet voice that can be spoken to our mind, spoken through circumstance, or spoken to us through observing people and nature.

To respect and understand who God is and what God is, is the beginning of divine knowledge. This is the starting point for realizing our destiny in God. Our carnal nature has to pass away, so that the spirit of Christ can grow and live through us. You cannot have an increase in love unless you have a diminishment of fear and disbelief.

The love of God surpasses knowledge, so once you grow enough in love, it goes beyond your human knowledge and causes you to seek God's knowledge. To gain God's knowledge, we have to stop seeing the world through human knowledge that focuses on our opinions and desires and start seeing the world from God's vantage point.

Only spiritual maturity will change your circumstances. When you come to a higher understanding, you realize you were born for a purpose. You are here to make a contribution and to make a difference.

This knowledge will start canceling a lot of insecurities. Fear begins to yield to love in controlling your actions. You're not afraid to say no in situations where you would normally say yes, because you want everyone to like you. You start becoming more comfortable with who you are. In realizing who you are, you begin to understand that there is a great power in this universe that guides you toward your unique destiny.

## "THE PRAYER OF LOVE" EMPHASIZING KNOWLEDGE

*And this I pray, that your love may abound <u>yet more and more in knowledge</u> and in all judgment; That ye may approve things that are excellent; that ye may be sincere and without offense till the day of Christ; Being filled with the fruits of righteousness, which are by Jesus Christ, unto the glory and praise of God.*

## POINT OF LOVE

*The desire for spiritual knowledge, in any form, is in essence a search for God.*

*God is love, therefore all knowledge we obtain about God will in one way or another increase our knowledge of love.*

# 4

## JUDGE FOR YOURSELF

*That Your Love May Grow
in All Judgment*

Love changes everything for the good and is proper in every circumstance. There is never a time when love is not the right thing to feel, and never a circumstance where it would be better not to love. Love has life. Love moves through people, awakening each one it touches to their divine potential.

Since love is living, it has the power to grow and to eventually displace anything that is contrary to it. Knowledge and judgment are the fertile fields into which love is sown, and from which appears a multiplying harvest of its precious and sought-after fruit.

To walk in unconditional love requires judgment. We are continually judging ourselves in ways we don't often think about, but learning how to judge or properly discern brings empowerment. Every day our maturity is being tested by the way we apply judgment. Judgment allows love to grow beyond any human conditions placed upon it.

When we use the word "judgment," we are not using it in the legal sense of pronouncing a verdict upon someone or their actions. Judgment is simply the ability to make a proper decision between two things. When we make judgments, we make a decision to do something or not to do it, to accept or to reject, to do good or to do evil, to help or to withhold help, to love or to hold back love, and to seek our divine connection or to remain as we are.

Judgment allows us to determine the desired direction of our life in relation to the lives of those around us. This is because proper judgment allows us to grow in love (my perspective of God) and knowledge (my perspective of myself as to who I am and why I'm here). Judgment, in this sense, is really discernment, which in the spiritual sense is the ability to know what is of God and what is not. Since God is love, then all decisions that come from this connection will be right.

We all seek to make the right decisions about our own lives. We desire to know what to do in every situation. How often do we make snap decisions based on emotion instead of properly discerning through understanding?

How we apply judgment is a measure of our growth in love. Respect, honor, humility, and submission are the true underpinnings of judgment.

Several years ago I was a presenter at a conference entitled "Spiritual Empowerment to Change Your World." I decided to survey the audience to see what they hoped to receive over the three days that we would be together. Some spoke of their desire for purpose, and others about using spiritual gifts, but at the heart of their comments, most wanted to achieve the elusive state of happiness.

Then I had them close their eyes, and I asked them three questions:

Do you tell your spouse and family members "I love you" on a daily basis?

Fewer than half raised their hands, and of those, the majority were women.

Do you say, "I love you" to anyone not a family member anytime during a regular week?

Only about 10 percent raised hands.

Do you find it awkward to tell other people, "I love you," or to give someone a hug?

The majority of the room raised their hands.

The theme of the conference was empowerment to change your world, yet this small survey showed that we have great difficulty in telling those in our world that we love them. We want to be happy, but at the root of what it is to be happy is a willingness to give and to receive love. Instead of finding happiness through loving relationships with others, many have substituted security through the accumulation of material possessions.

When we say, "I love you," or give someone an endearing embrace, we put ourselves in a vulnerable position if our expression of love is not returned. It is usually safer just to keep our distance, but it always limits our ability to draw closer and establish meaningful relationships. Discerning how to give and how to accept gestures of love is a powerful tool in establishing relationships. We choose to be defensive instead of vulnerable, but this is due to a lack of proper judgment or discernment.

# LOVE REQUIRES JUDGMENT

Judgment is directly related to the exercise of love and knowledge. If I am able to make proper judgments about myself, I do not have to be defensive.

If I am able to make proper judgments about others, I don't have to reject others. Much of what is considered poor judgment is a manifestation of emotion. People do things in the heat of the moment. They exercise poor judgment; they make decisions they shouldn't make. And these things start compounding.

Love is a perception of God. Knowledge is a perception of myself as I am connected to God. And judgment is the reaction that happens between love and knowledge, and changes how I do what I do, why I go where I go, why I talk like I talk. It allows me to make better decisions, because I see myself from a perspective that other people are not privy to.

So judgment is the ability to make good choices in my life, because I realize I'm part of God's universe, part of a greater plan. I know who I am, so I'm not ashamed of myself. My actions and my attitudes submitted to judgment will bring forth responsibility.

I love Little League baseball. I love apple pie with ice cream. I love this country. I love the warming rays of sunshine on a crisp autumn morning. I love success. I love to run on the beach. I love my new car. I love Europe. I love winning. I love my wife. We use the word "love" in a wide variety of situations. Unlike some languages that have different words for love depending on the context, in English one word covers all.

When we really like something, we often say, "I love it." Love means many different things to different people, and there are many things that mask themselves as love. Liking things, being passionate about things, being infatuated with or lustful toward another person——none of these imitations of love offer us real love, the most basic need that any of us has. If we can discern the kind of love that God brings to our life, we can see these imitations for what they are.

*Proper judgment is divine discernment. For love to grow in judgment you must learn to see as God sees.*

Just as food and clothing are vital for physical survival, so love is required for emotional well-being and spiritual life. The greatest imprisonment any of us can experience is to be isolated from love. Discernment as to how we deal with the issue of love will give us much insight on our actions and attitudes.

When we are isolated from love, we seek these substitutes. In an effort to mitigate the pain of not receiving what is so vitally needed for our spiritual survival, we build walls of indifference, human judgment, and rejection. Since these protective attitudes and actions are a manifestation of our hidden and often misunderstood fear, the higher we build the walls, the harder it becomes to give or receive love.

## LOVE SUBSTITUTES

Just as we have false imitations of love, we find ourselves wooed by substitutes for being loved. The need for attention is a love substitute, as is a craving for acceptance. The desire for sympathy is also a surrogate for love. The insatiable hunger for praise is likewise an overwhelming appeal for love. We all know people who continually position themselves in the limelight. They have to be at the center of everything that is happening. There are others who are continually in a "woe is me" attitude, and still others who will do or say almost anything so that people will receive them or think well of them. If we look closely at ourselves, we will probably recognize some of these needs within ourselves as well.

Childhood is a time of learning and growing into maturity. From the time of birth and even in the womb, we are seeking affection, security, and love. When we have a need, we cry—it is a normal cry to be accepted and loved. A child who is constantly disruptive and seeking attention is probably insecure about whether he or she is loved. When a child scrapes her knee and whimpers, she is trying to attract sympathy for her pain, so she can be reassured that someone cares and is willing to help. We've all seen children who are old enough to know better but will do almost any act to get others to notice and extend praise.

If you think about it, many adults do similar things. These actions are not necessarily improper, depending on our maturity level. They are expressions of our need to receive love. They are part of being human and growing spiritually. If the response to our attention-grabbing, sympathy-longing, praise-seeking childish actions is love or loving discipline, then we mature and learn to give and grow in love in these situations.

If, however, we are criticized, castigated, yelled at for

being a baby, reprimanded for not growing up, or otherwise ridiculed, we will acquire fear.

These fears do not magically disappear when we reach the age of eighteen or twenty-one, but stay with us until such times as the power of love through God and others eliminates our various fears. This is why we need to seek and acquire spiritual maturity through "The Prayer of Love," because His power allows us to overcome all fear by partaking of His nature.

If we don't learn to walk in spiritual maturity, we will forever be captives of our fears. A correction, physical or otherwise, delivered to a child in love will always bring growth and deliverance from potentially harmful attitudes. The same correction delivered in anger or as a means of dominating the child will yield more fear and, if continually repeated, eventually rebellion.

When we engage in immature conversation and actions—and who of us has not?—is it possible we are acting out of fears that have not been perfected by love? When we crave continuous attention or sympathy or continual praise, is it possible that what we are really seeking is love? Spiritual maturity will deliver us from fear by giving us the understanding and ability to walk in love.

Spiritual judgment or discernment will reveal many

signs of our need to be perfected in love. The fear of rejection is the king of all fears. As adults we protect ourselves from rejection in various ways.

Monopolizing conversations through continuous talking, vigorously avoiding confrontation, yielding to peer pressure, and prejudicial attitudes toward others—all can be responses to our fear of rejection. Only discerning divine love can deliver us from these.

*Judgment or divine discernment brings understanding. It allows you to face your fears head-on with courage and anticipation.*

As you pray "let my love abound in all judgment," God will reveal to you your insecurities and the reasons you act and think as you do. You will gain freedom by allowing your attitudes and actions to become judged in the light of who you really are, and not by your fears. As you pray "let my love abound in all judgment," God will also reveal your spiritual nature and unique personality. These are usually obscured, but become revealed in the light of His truth. Our ministry, gifting, vision, inheritance, purpose, and destiny are all things to be discerned.

God's love will set us totally free. This love always comes to us in peace. It never produces fear. Divine love works in every circumstance. It always sees as God sees. That is, it always sees the best in every situation. It always looks for the good and is not eager to uncover wrong. It never condemns us or makes demands of us, but is patient to allow us to change. This is how we can discern love, as opposed to its counterfeits.

## THE STRUGGLE WITHIN

Loving myself does not mean approving of or overlooking negative character issues or poor habits. As humans, we have both soul and spirit. These are tightly interconnected and though they are different, together they affect our personality and our nature. The spirit is that which knows God and comes from God. The soul is composed of our mind, will, and emotions. These two can be at odds with each other.

As the Apostle Paul said in commenting on the opposition of these two within each of us, "What I want to do that I don't do but what I don't want, that I do." Haven't we all felt this way? We desire to act a certain way, but have such a hard time doing it. For example, my intention was to keep quiet, but when she said that or when he did that, "I just couldn't help myself, I had to give them a piece of my mind" or "I couldn't let them get away with that." Afterward we say things like "Why couldn't I just keep my big mouth shut?" or "Why was I so stupid?" or "I must be the biggest idiot in the whole world." Sound familiar? Sure it does, we've all had encounters that we've regretted.

Sometimes we are made to feel guilty for saying or doing the right thing. Unless we have proper judgment, we have no way of discerning if our actions were appropriate or if they were out of bounds.

Our spirit desires to do the God thing rooted in love, but the carnal mind of our soul desires its own thing, rooted in pride and fear. When our carnal mind (the mind of our animal passions and instincts) gets us into trouble, it brings us pain and embarrassment.

We often accuse ourselves and get angry with ourselves. Sometimes the hardest person to forgive is ourself. Our spirit needs to forgive our mind (soul). This is what forgiving yourself means. Your spirit that knows God and has been so often overpowered and embarrassed by the will of the soul needs to forgive the soul just like it would forgive another person. This releases your soul to change. If your spirit——your desire to do right and seek your divine connection—is constantly at war with your soul, it is difficult to be at peace or to live above circumstances.

To grow spiritually, we must learn to grow in our communication with God. God is always speaking. God speaks through people, through circumstances, through writings, through nature, in science, in history, in dreams, and in our thoughts. God's methods of communication are boundless.

## GOD LIKES TO TALK

God desires to talk and is constantly speaking, but we need to train ourselves to hear. When I pray "let my love abound in all judgment," I am also seeking a discernment that will allow me to hear God in ever-clearer ways. This prayer asks God to make me ever-more aware of His voice.

Just as radio waves are continually carrying sound and pictures through the air, so God is continually speaking. To receive a radio transmission, we must have a receiver that is tuned in to the proper frequency. To hear God, we must become tuned in to the manner in which He communicates—through people, by nature, in circumstances, and within our spirit.

The design and order of nature communicates to us constantly, and since we come from God, our spirits are able to sense and know this voice. Since many of us have not understood our creation in God's image, we are in need of having our spiritual senses exercised to discern what is of God and what is in opposition to Him.

There is a language of the spirit, and it is the communication of love. As with any natural language, such as French, mathematics, or poetry, there is a requirement that we learn the grammar and patterns of the language, and the art of interpretation, in order to become able to comprehend what is being expressed. To be aware that we are spiritual beings in natural bodies with the ability to know and hear God is the beginning of discernment.

*For where your treasure is,*
*there will your heart be also.*
—Luke 12:34 (The Amplified Bible)

There is a vast group of people who are frustrated, thinking that to really grow in spirituality and make a difference, they must become something different from what they already are. They sometimes equate religious positions with spirituality. Spirituality and walking with God are not limited to a building or even a specific religion. God has placed eternity, a divine treasure, in each person's heart. This treasure is like gold, veined among the rocks. It needs to be discovered, mined, and processed.

People often plan their future or seek direction without ever considering that God has already placed within them the seeds of their possibility and destiny. When you walk in judgment, you realize that you already possess all that is necessary through Christ.

Jesus was giving us a window on discerning our destiny when he uttered the words "for where your treasure is, there your heart will be also." If you want to find your spiritual treasure, then you must go on a treasure hunt. If you reverse Jesus' words, you will find the location of your spiritual riches. For where your heart is, there your treasure will be also. So you'll find your spiritual identity, inheritance, purpose, and destiny (treasure) by looking into your heart.

Often people never realize that their manner of contributing to society was divinely placed. Many are frustrated and feel they are at a dead end, because they are pursuing directions contrary to their heart.

Consider your dreams as a child. Perhaps you dreamt of flying airplanes, perhaps you liked all things athletic. A child may continually play at being a doctor or police officer, caring for and helping people, while another may be constantly building things out of any material he can find. These traits, though they can be encouraged or suppressed, are inborn. What is being acted out is from the heart, and finds its source in the divine purpose. The number one way we as humans work to progress society is through our occupation.

Think of how society often directs its members to find employment based on the amount of money the job pays, or on the ease of the work, or because it is a high-profile or admired position. No wonder surveys show that the majority of workers, even those with high-paying jobs, are dissatisfied with their employment choice. Most people never realize that their occupation is spiritual. That is why to be content and at peace, we must seek out our heart and find our divinely ordained purpose. When we do this, we will find that our occupation becomes our vocation.

## His Work Becomes Our Occupation

An occupation is the type of work that occupies our energies and abilities, as we work together as a society for our joint survival and advancement. A vocation is how I use my occupation as a spiritual instrument for the betterment of humankind and the fulfillment of my divine purpose.

We are spiritual beings and partakers of the divine nature. Although some are called to be leaders within a religion, we all are ministers of spiritual things. To discern my vocation, as an operation of my divine purpose and destiny, gives me direction and a freedom to be me and to be comfortable with the way I was made.

*To live with a deficit of love causes pain. Our heart is always full. If it is not filled with love, it will be filled with pain.*

There is an art to maturing mentally and maintaining the attributes of innocence and kindness. It really is an understanding of who I am and the value of who I am in God. That knowledge in itself—that I am not alone, that none of us are a-lone entity or an island, that we are all connected to one another, that we are all part of one another—gives us power to change. So in essence, for God to manifest fully, we must come corporately together as humanity.

The Bible instructs that the heavens declare the glory of God, and invisible things from the creation are clearly seen by the things that are made. In other words, the ultimate end of all human knowledge and accomplishment should be to bring instruction to us about God.

Normal children, because of innocence, do not live life with the hang-ups of so many of their adult counterparts. They do not possess great human knowledge, but their innocence allows them to demonstrate many divine attributes. When you look at little infants, there is nothing threatening about them. They lack knowledge, and they lack the ability to reject or cause harm. That is one reason everyone finds them so loveable, because they are totally nonintimidating. Only when people grow into adulthood without growing in love, do they become threatening to others.

*The language of the spirit is the language of love. You can learn to receive His love constantly and thus hear His voice continually.*

In our attitudes and actions, we are not to be children but to become like children. Little children make up easily. They do not hold grudges. They desire to interact and have fun with others. They want to believe all things. They try to be helpful. They lack disguises and speak directly. They love to be loved, and to give and receive hugs and kisses. Discerning how to become like a child is a key to learning to love.

There have been many wise and sacrificial individuals throughout history who have sought to point humankind toward spirituality. These were not perfect human beings, and certainly many of their followers adversely modified their teachings and altered their intentions.

Humankind is on a God quest to find spirituality. This desire, unfortunately, often manifests itself in strange and peculiar ways, and in bizarre teachings.

No one possesses all knowledge or understands all the ways of God. Finding a fuller connection to our spirituality is a key that will help each of us.

## YOUR ROADMAP FOR SPIRITUAL TRANSFORMATION

There has been no greater teacher of life principles and spiritual transformation than Jesus Christ. Though many of his followers have altered his words and even subverted his intentions, his teachings form a roadmap for spiritual transformation.

If we can separate what Jesus taught from what some of his present-day followers teach about him, we will find the foundation for loving others. Jesus taught that he (what he was and what he possessed) was the way, the truth, and the life, leading to God. His close followers reasserted this affirmation by stating that there was no other name than that of Jesus that was able to deliver humankind from its opposition to God and reconnect the world to Him. These and other biblical themes have become ritualized by some in an attempt to coax individuals into following their particular brand of religion.

The reason Jesus could say that he was the way to God was because he was the perfect manifestation of love in human form. The Gospels demonstrate that he learned obedience to love by the things he suffered and was literally one with God. His life, death, and resurrection are a pattern for us to follow in our journey toward greater love.

As the Apostle Paul taught, Jesus is the only name that could deliver us from our carnal nature (the mind of our animal passions and instincts) into our divine destiny. In biblical teachings, a person's name is synonymous with his nature. When a person had a change in their nature, they often received a name change. Such was the case of one named Jacob (which means "one who deceives"). When he had an encounter with God, his nature was changed along with his name, which became Israel, meaning "one who has power with God."

When we are delivered from the things that oppose God, it comes by learning to take on the same nature that Jesus had. It is the only way. We love as he loved. We talk as he talked. We think as he thought. We become as he is. His divine nature becomes our nature, as we are shaped to have the character of Christ. Discerning this gives us our pattern, our empowerment, and our ultimate salvation.

## "THE PRAYER OF LOVE" EMPHASIZING PROPER JUDGMENT

*And this I pray, that your love may abound yet more and more in knowledge <u>and in all judgment;</u> That ye may approve things that are excellent; that ye may be sincere and without offense till the day of Christ; Being filled with the fruits of righteousness, which are by Jesus Christ, unto the glory and praise of God.*

# POINT OF LOVE

......................................................

*We are told by Jesus to judge not lest we be judged.*

*To be able to have the same perception of others as we have of ourself is one of love's greatest attributes.*

*When we use a different set of criteria to form our opinions of the actions and words of others than we use in forming opinions about ourself, we reveal a spiritual weakness within our character.*

*True equality is found in measuring to others the same love we give ourself.*

# 5

## TAKING POSSESSION OF EXCELLENT THINGS

### Approving Things That Are Excellent

Appreciation is a wonderful thing:
It makes what is excellent in others belong to us as well.

—VOLTAIRE

In the fourth benchmark of "The Prayer of Love," you will learn to pray that you may approve the things that are excellent. In approving excellence, we learn to utilize knowledge and judgment as a means of growing in love.

All things that come from God are excellent. All people seek to be "happy," but not all seek the excellence that can bring them to a contented state. Joy, peace, patience, courage, strength, insight, integrity, virtue, and the like don't just happen but are a byproduct of spiritual maturity. You need a process to prove in yourself the effectiveness of these excellent things in order to possess them as your own.

Approving excellence is proving in yourself the value and effectiveness of allowing excellent things to change and shape your attitude and actions. Only when you have approved excellence are you able to properly deal with character traits that hinder excellence and, thus, limit love.

If you were at sea at night in a small boat and a massive storm approached, you would need a means of determining your location so that you could safely navigate toward shore. A compass, a radio, sea charts, or even a lighted landmark could all be of help in pointing you toward safe harbor. Unless you could determine where you were on the water in relation to where land was, it would be impossible to find direction.

As we navigate life, the benchmarks contained in Paul's prayer help us to locate where we are, who we are, and how we can change. They give us a means of progressing from a purely human nature toward the nature of God. Without benchmarks, we are adrift without a means of direction to help us find our divine destiny. Approving excellence is where the width of the benchmark funnel significantly narrows.

This fourth benchmark is the place where knowledge and judgment that is rooted in love become applied to our lives. All the knowledge in the world and an understanding of how to utilize it are of little consequence, unless it is actually applied in such a way as to bring desired change.

Approving excellence is the quest to find God in all things. In God are perfect love, order, function, understanding, application, operation, peace, and more. When we strive for the better way, "the God way," it produces excellence.

## A LOVE FABLE

There once was a small town, and in that town was a ferocious lion that had been captured and put on display, being chained in the square. The lion existed on waste scraps thrown his way. Continually he tried to break free, but to no avail, for the chains were far too strong.

The townspeople would walk by and laugh at this once proud king of the jungle and mock his condition. In one of the lion's fits to gain freedom, he struck his paw against the side of the tree to which he was chained and got a large sliver.

The bleeding of his swelled paw brought little sympathy from the onlookers. Then one night a young maiden, who was often derided and belittled by the townsfolk, decided to see if she could remove the sliver from the lion. She had always felt bad about the way the lion had been treated and could no longer bear to see the lion suffer.

Late one evening she approached the fearless beast with caution, for she knew he would be able to destroy her with one powerful sweep of his forearm. As she drew near, she calmed the lion, telling him that she only wanted to remove the sliver from his paw.

As she carefully removed the sliver from the swollen paw, the lion spoke: "I am the king of the land, and my kingdom has suffered much from the people of this village. I allowed myself to be captured to see if there was anyone within the village who possessed even a measure of kindness before I brought destruction upon everyone who lives here."

The next day the village awoke surrounded by lions and elephants and all the beasts of the land. When they came to the square, they saw the lion free with the young maiden by his side. He said, "Except for the kindness shown by this girl, your entire village would be trampled down and not one of you would escape, but she pleaded for your lives and therefore I have spared you."

When she embraced the lion as he was about to depart, he said to her, "Remember, love is always found just on the other side of your fear, and in seeking to do an excellent thing, you have delivered your neighbors."

## MATURITY IS MARKED
## BY EXCELLENCE

Whether we are developing manned flight to Mars, preparing to win an athletic contest, cleaning the house, looking to solve world hunger, developing a better pencil, or seeking to grow in maturity and attain our destiny, a desire for excellence is what characterizes the outcome. Seeking the God-way of understanding and doing all things will increasingly lead toward a more excellent way of being and doing.

In the early days of human flight, inventors worked with a limited knowledge of aerodynamics. Some, from at least as far back as Leonardo da Vinci, discerned from studying the flight of birds that utilizing a wing and its curvature were required principles if men were to fly.

These innovators repeatedly applied the knowledge and understanding they had to produce a wide variety of designs that, though lacking in their ability to produce flight, were incremental steps toward achieving human aviation. With each attempt came an enhanced knowledge and an increased discernment of how to better change and adapt their designs.

*People are constantly measuring their value or success by others. We can only truly measure ourselves by God's standard.*

There were many unworkable ideas and some brilliant refinements birthed out of a quest for excellence. Eventually the Wright Brothers, through the proper application of knowledge and discernment, were able to bring forth the excellence of human flight.

All advancement requires the approving of excellence. In the context of this writing, it means that at some point your knowledge and discernment must have a means of impacting and changing your life. It is through approving excellence that we learn how to utilize knowledge and discernment so that through the power of love, they become instruments to propel us toward our divine destiny.

The first or outer rim of our lives (the funnel) is love, and it affects everything else. It affects how we acquire and use knowledge, and it affects our judgment.

Your sincerity and your offense can be measured by the depth and character of your love. This is because love is what changes your feelings about your personal worth and about people. Love is the only force that is able to change your human perceptions, rooted in opinion and formed by experience into a divine perception.

So with abounding love, the bigger your love gets, the more you are able to deal with all the other issues of life. Love is the foundation; it is the beginning and end of our pursuit. Knowledge works by love, and judgment works by love. All things work by love. All things.

When we get down to approving things that are excellent, it would seem easy for us to see things that we think are good and call them excellent. This is not what is meant by approving excellence. To approve excellence is to prove yourself according to a godly standard and thereby do the things that are excellent.

## YOUR DESTINY IS IN GOD'S NATURE

We each have a destiny that can be known and completed if we allow ourselves to become progressively changed toward God's nature. We begin to approve excellence when we are able, because of our attitude and desire to increase in love.

Love, knowledge, and judgment allow us to draw a distinction between what is good and bad, right and wrong, what we should or should not do. How we should or should not respond. Our capacity to overcome negative habits and character traits hinges, or pivots, upon our ability to understand and work toward excellence. Approving excellence can be likened to a teeter-totter. You walk in love, knowledge, and judgment, and then the pivotal thing that tips the scales toward action is approving excellence.

We have to be able to approve things that we know to

be excellent, regardless of how nonexcellent or how pitiful situations are. In our search to approve excellence, we gain the capacity to become sincere in all things, to overcome all offense, and to acquire fruits of righteousness.

This requires faith. Faith is the pivotal point. Approving excellence requires a divine faith. In order to approve excellence, we must see things from the divine perspective and act on what we see.

Faith is not some unsupportable hope or a mental exercise that produces change if you repeat your desires long enough and loudly enough and claim them ardently enough. Some people treat faith as though, if they refuse, by mental resolve, to entertain thoughts contrary to their desired expectation and if they fervently advance the things they desire, then they will have those things. This is mind or soul power, but it can never produce a faith that approves excellence. Genuine faith is to understand and apply truth. This truth starts to come to us as we seek God's will and discover our preordained purpose in God.

Faith requires understanding of the godly purpose and nature in all things. If we understand the truth, then we no longer see ourselves and others according to the evidence of human failings and weaknesses. Rather, seeing with the eyes of faith allows us to see past and present circumstances and into divine possibility.

Some people who have a love for their children lack knowledge or have poor judgment. They may slap them around, treat them in a gruff manner, correct them at the wrong times, and embarrass them in front of people because they lack discernment. They cannot approve excellence because their love has not grown in knowledge and judgment. They have no idea of who they or their children are or why they inhabit the earth at this time. They have no plan for a future beyond their mortality because no one has ever shown them their divine destiny.

Their immaturity keeps them blind to their true potential. So they wander aimlessly pursuing human comforts at the expense of direction and purpose.

## You Are an Essential Piece of God's Plan

I was really born to be me. That is where my destiny lies. If I can really understand it, if I can grasp a vision of who I am to be in my divine purpose and stop trying to be something or someone else, then I can begin to work toward that goal. Excellence is not reaching someone else's goal for me; it is reaching the goal that I was born to achieve.

I was not destined to be Isaac Newton, so I should not shoot myself between the eyes because I can't do math. I was not born to be Jane Austen, so I should not become frustrated with my inability to write a romantic story set in a backdrop of human tension, intrigue, and suspense. I was not supposed to be Martin Luther King, Jr., so why should I find my inability to communicate and move the masses toward acceptance and social change so perplexing?

If I sing with the voice of a foghorn rather than that of a songbird, why would I desire to be Carrie Underwood or Frank Sinatra? If we knew who we really were, we would learn from other people rather than trying to become them.

If we really knew who we were in God, then we would understand that our destiny is as great and significant to the divine purpose as any of those mentioned above. My peace and prominence is not in material accusation or notoriety, but in awareness and completion of my unique divine destiny.

The wise don't fall into the trap of seeking fame and fortune above that of destiny. They comprehend that only being who they were meant to be can bring real peace and lasting influence.

Unfortunately, many individuals of renown attained their position by seeking to imitate the "success" of the famous and never have found destiny. Not being aware of the possibility of divine identity and acceptance, they seek a fleeting human substitute.

What distinguishes many of us from them is not notoriety or ability, but an understanding of our destiny and how to achieve it. The greatest spiritual achievers may seldom come up on the radar screen of the world's most famous and influential people, but if they have learned how to find and walk toward their destiny, their impact upon eternal things is as great as any.

People who fail to recognize their own vital importance and wondrous uniqueness seek fame over destiny and usually obtain neither.

You can absolutely find something wrong with everyone. So excellence is not trying to be what everybody thinks you should be or changing yourself according to others' expectations. It is also not trying to get everyone else to be what you think they ought to be or to have others fulfill your expectations.

# PROVE YOURSELF EXCELLENT

Excellence is marked by simply coming into a peaceful and a serene satisfaction of who you are and being able to live it. Becoming comfortable with who you are and what you can achieve is the source of great peace and allows you to grow. Anyone can look at something that is good and say, "It's good, I like it." To be able to look at something that is not necessarily a finished product and say, "It's going to be all right, I can see what it is destined to be," requires faith. Faith allows you to approve something that in its present state is lacking, but because faith allows you to see the finished work, you can approve it in its excellent state.

When you get to that point, you are able to tip the scale the other way and start working with sincerity, offense, and the fruits of righteousness. Faith is where all this is going to work, because you have to have faith to be sincere and to be delivered from offenses. We have to believe that this prayer will change us. We have to have faith for that because those are things that by ourselves, we can't really change. I cannot change myself or I would already have done so. Therefore, if I can't approve excellence or see a finished product, then I will usually be blind to my condition while at the same time unable to overlook the faults of others.

At some point I have to be willing to work on myself, and that is where I see my love, knowledge, and judgment approving excellence. If I can get to that point, I am able to see a finished product and have faith in God rather than in things.

Then I may, through my faith, be able to move the mountains of self-delusion, not in fear or in offense or even from hurt, but in understanding and in love. Wounded people have arrows targeted for my heart. I am able to see beyond their lack of kindness because of my faith. Faith sees the unseen. It allows me to start dealing with life not with what I see in natural circumstances, but with eyes of faith in divine possibility to make all things good and right. As Marie Curie, the two-time Nobel Prize winner, said, "Nothing in life is to be feared, it is only to be understood. Now is the time to understand more, so that we may fear less." Seeking to approve excellence allows you to understand yourself more and fear less.

One manifestation of fear is rejection stemming from a carnal desire for other people's approval. The opposite of rejection is a love and acceptance of yourself—self-approval. This is a love of who you are and not an acceptance of your negative actions and attitudes. Loving and approving of yourself means that you feel safe, worthy, and acceptable. God loves us and has always loved us. Although things contrary to His divine nature—anger, malice, dishonesty, self-seeking, etc.—are not accepted, God's love for us does not diminish because we practice such behavior.

Rather, practicing such behavior diminishes our ability to receive and understand divine love. It hinders our potential in God.

## MOMENT OF EMPOWERMENT

You are empowered at the present time to reshape your future by your choice of thoughts. Change takes place at the point you connect your thoughts to the present moment of opportunity. The moment of empowerment is now, the present. It is not lost in your past failures or a moment to be reached in your future—your empowerment is always in the present moment. Therefore the convergence of possibility opens new doors for you, and a brand new beginning. You can refuse to change the way you think and remain living in your problems, or you can choose better thoughts and live the good life—the God life. Either way, it remains your choice. So if you don't like your life, change it.

By praying "let me approve the things that are excellent," you allow God to bring forth His character in you. Instead of trying to bring it to pass in your human efforts, God empowers you to do it supernaturally.

Allow your thoughts to shift from not being good enough, smart enough, thin enough, rich enough, spiritual enough, etc., by releasing your feeling of being wrong. That means you eliminate self-criticism, unworthiness, and rejection—receiving divine transformation by believing only the truth resident in God's divine nature.

*Faith is not blind belief. The longing of your heart for love gives you a desire for reality and a belief that in the evidence of love you can find and live in your God nature.*

You may feel that you are living from crisis to crisis, with problems galore. You need to stay away from the thoughts that created the problem in the first place. Love, through knowledge and proper discernment (judgment), will, through God's power, change this moment by changing the way you think so that you behave differently and ultimately live a life of purpose, peace, and prosperity. The love you have is found in your thoughts before it ever manifests in your experiences. Every crisis in your life is an external result of an internal thought and can be an opportunity for change. Your willingness to let go of your old ways of thinking is key to creating a better life for yourself.

If our motive is to let go in order to achieve happiness or position, it will produce limited benefit. This is why self-help techniques are always at a loss to bring lasting and life-altering change. However, if our motive is love, then the power of God, who is love, brings the change almost effortlessly. To deal with only the external symptoms is a waste of your time and energy—your thoughts and perceptions must change first before you can release the need for resistance.

Anger is a frustration at things not being the way you think they should be or the refusal to perceive life in a new or different way. If you habitually respond to every conflict with anger, you never learn a better solution to your problems. Life becomes a cycle of irritation and disappointment because you refuse to change the thoughts that created the problem. Getting upset doesn't answer your problem; it just postpones the lesson for a future time. The present is the only time you can deal with your anger.

Some may not like the possible outcome to their conflict and respond by just "giving up"—quitting because they think there is nothing that can be done. It's hopeless, so why even try? Some blame others, but blame is a snare that will keep you forever bound. If you are blaming someone else for your predicament, it means you are not taking responsibility for yourself. Resentment, criticism, and guilt come from blaming others. You cannot approve excellence if you feel someone else is to blame for your problems. People at times do wrong us, but to become consumed with anger or resentment toward them keeps us bound. What we need to do is allow love, through divine knowledge and proper judgment, to release us from our attitudes that have entrapped us via our negative emotions.

## The Counterbalance of Change

Your willingness to change is the counterbalance to your stubbornness and resistance. You may want your life to become better or easier, but it won't happen if you're expecting the change to come through someone else. It is precisely when you feel resistance to change that you need God to change you the most—that's why you fight against it so intently. Your resistance is evidenced in self-righteousness (blaming others), anger (attacking any opposition), or withdrawing yourself (reluctance, procrastination, or just quitting).

A proceeding word is a current word spoken by God that is relevant for your present situation. If you are not looking for the proceeding word from God, you can never really grow up. The Apostle Paul put this so eloquently when he wrote, "When I was a child, I spake as a child, I understood as a child, I thought as a child; but when I became a man, I put away childish things" (1 Corinthians 13:11). Continually living out how you feel or how you were mistreated produces childish thoughts, temper tantrums, and reluctance. Maturity is the grateful attitude, which produces a desire to love and to find destiny that transforms your thoughts into divine thoughts.

Impatience is just another form of resistance. You feel justified that you do not have the time to learn the lesson involved with the problem you created—oftentimes getting angry, so you don't have to deal with it at all. Yet God brings it back to you again at another, opportune time. Learning to pray "I want to approve the things that are excellent" overcomes our self-imposed limitations. Everything that you are unwilling to release is a limitation that restricts your growth and potential.

Seek to approve excellence so that you don't make excuses or justify why you don't need to change. As the Apostle Paul pointed out in Romans 2:4, religious people and the immature despised the riches of His goodness . . . not knowing that the goodness of God leads to repentance—godly change. In other words, our immaturity or religious viewpoints can hinder our ability to receive God's goodness by our unwillingness to accept godly change.

Salvation is not just about your eternal reward, it is an incredible gift of wholeness in every dimension, right now, if you are willing to receive it. God's mercy releases us from the past to fulfill His purpose and destiny.

## Becoming the Express Image

Awareness is the first step to shifting our thoughts and perceptions. If you have a behavioral pattern hidden deep within, you must become aware of your habit in order to change it. When it is brought to your attention, you choose whether to remain as you are or to change. Love through divine knowledge and proper judgment brings awareness, but it is approving excellence that brings the change.

Divine grace is able to come to you wherever you are, and to bring light and direction. In grace is a power for forgiveness that can open emotional doors you may have kept locked for years. Not only can you release others by forgiveness, but forgiveness releases you from a self-imposed prison as well. It is imperative to release yourself from your past. Forgiveness is letting go of your history. Forgiveness releases the cycle of reliving the past experiences to finally walk through the doors of present empowerment.

God gives you profound peace to transform your life, peace that means coming into divine order and harmony. His peace activates your potential—it is the power within to transform every thought into creative expressions.

If the whole essence of life is to become the express image of the divine purpose, then transition and change are crucial for success. Your degree of resistance to accepting this transition is the measure of your willingness to change. The more resistance, the less maturity you have in an area.

A willing heart offers tremendous opportunity and significance. It means you have no resistance to putting away childish thoughts to grow up in Him . . . no resistance to maturing in Christ . . . and no resistance to changing your agenda to fulfill His. Learning to overcome resistance is the master key to approving excellence in your life. As a wire heats up when it is resistant to the electricity flowing through it, so when we are resistant to approving excellence, we become heated and upset through fear, anger, and frustration.

When you pray to approve the things that are excellent, you allow God to bring forth your strengths and your purpose. You become focused on solutions and not problems. You acquire a more outward view because abounding love, knowledge, and judgment work in you through excellence to turn you toward others. Once you start approving excellence, you start growing in your perception of God and your value to Him.

In approving excellence, you seek to find not only the good, but you search for what is better. Love, knowledge, and judgment come first in the funnel, because they give you a perspective that is from God. In order to change the things that are inside, you must have a perspective that comes from outside yourself.

What happens in the first three benchmarks of "The Prayer of Love" is that I gain the capacity for internal growth and change, and then when I start approving excellence, the last three benchmarks allow me to perfect my attitudes and actions toward others. The first three benchmarks focus on my relationship with God, while the last three benchmarks—sincerity, offense, and fruits of righteousness—allow me to deal with hindrances in my relationships with others.

Approving excellence is the pivotal point (the fourth benchmark) that allows my God-focus to become directed toward others.

## "THE PRAYER OF LOVE" FOCUSING ON APPROVING EXCELLENCE

*And this I pray, that your love may abound yet more and more in knowledge and in all judgment; That ye may approve things that are excellent; that ye may be sincere and without offense till the day of Christ; Being filled with the fruits of righteousness, which are by Jesus Christ, unto the glory and praise of God.*

# POINT OF LOVE

*Where you find exceptional love you will usually find people who were greatly blessed and who also suffered significant loss.*

*The blessing of love is revealed in peace, fulfillment, and appreciation; yet without becoming victorious over the episodes of loss we've experienced, the depth of our blessing would be less astounding.*

# 6

## WHEN THE WAX IS TAKEN AWAY

*That You May Be Sincere*

Abraham Lincoln was fond of telling this story: There was a wise king who lived in the land. His wisdom was legendary, and people would come from far and wide to ask him questions and seek his understanding. No question was ever too great; no riddle was too hard to answer. So all the learned men of the kingdom got together to see if they could come up with a question that would stump their ruler. After much deliberation, they asked the king the following:

"Oh great king, tell us a statement that is useful and

true in every situation, whether that situation be good or evil, great or small, or if it be one of joy or sorrow."

As the king pondered the request, they mused with excitement, thinking, "At last we have stumped the king."

Then the king spoke and said these words: "This too shall pass away."

Love is the only eternal thing in the universe—all else will pass away. If you can see the big picture by seeing yourself outside of your current circumstances, it will give you boldness and sincerity to always love.

Love, divine knowledge, proper discernment, and a willingness to bring forth excellence have brought you to the place where insincerity and offense can be overcome. Insincerity, offense, and a lack of righteousness are the great stumbling blocks to discovering and growing in love. Sincerity is at the narrow end of our spiritual funnel. The benchmarks of "The Prayer of Love" are in a particular order—without establishing the first four benchmarks, it will be impossible to overcome the obstacles to developing strong, healthy relationships with all people. The final three benchmarks, beginning with sincerity, will help us develop properly in character.

*To be sincere is not something you do but something you are.*

The greatest anxiety and distress that befall each of us are not rooted in life's many unforeseen struggles, but rather in the unending conflict of the mind. Though we often try to escape from unpleasant thoughts, they have no off-button. The most we can do with the unwelcome thoughts, it seems, is to cover them up with activity and sleep. However, proper character helps us channel thoughts into productive and fulfilling areas. Our loneliness is most apparent when we fail to express our thoughts due to a fear of having them rejected or even scorned by others.

## IS IT ABOUT ME OR THEM?

My parents met at a tent meeting. My mother was orphaned as a young teenager and raised by a kind lady whom she met only once prior to coming to live with her. One night on the back porch, my mother heard music coming from a nearby field and followed the sound. My father was the young minister helping that night, and in that tent in the middle of a farm field began not only a lifelong romance but also a lifelong effort to help people, especially those who had great needs.

Perhaps my parents' greatest attribute was that they genuinely loved people and had dedicated their lives to helping others. My father started twenty-seven churches, so we moved often. We usually moved into an old house that was in need of much repair, and by the time we got it in livable condition, we'd be on the move again.

My mother was amazing, and I saw her cry only once about material possessions. It was time to start another church, and as usual, we put most of our furniture up for sale. I remember my mother sitting on the couch and crying because we couldn't take it with us and had to sell it. She said to my father, "Honey, are you sure we need to move?" and as soon as he said, "Francis, we're needed in the next town," she wiped her eyes, and they were off again.

They had sincerity. They were genuine, or as the expression goes, they were the real deal.

Success can sometimes cloud sincerity. I've seen it many times. In human terms, I had success at an early age. Preaching to thousands of people, being in constant demand, having a network offer to put me on national television—all could have been in opposition to the sixth benchmark of the Apostle Paul's prayer. But what kept me on the mark was my parents' selfless example. I would often hear my father say to me, "Mark, you must always ask yourself, Am I here because of me, or am I here because of them?" If you're in life for yourself, you can have human success, but spiritual success is built on being sincere with other people and most of all with yourself. Each person has a great destiny, but it can only come to pass in an atmosphere of sincerity.

To truly love all people requires sincerity.

We live in a world that is abundant in possessions and impoverished by a growing lack of love. Sincerity is a commodity in very short supply in most relationships. By flattery, manipulation, and disingenuous praise, people seek to gain material advantage at the expense of genuine relationship.

The word "sincere" as cited in folk etymology suggests that it is derived from the Latin *sine*, meaning "without," and *cera*, meaning "wax." The story is told of how dishonest potters or sculptors in Roman times would use wax to cover up flaws in order to deceive the purchaser; thus "sincere," meaning "without wax," would denote honesty and genuineness. The wise purchaser of a piece could test whether or not it was genuine by holding it next to fire to see if any wax melted out.

*That the trial of your faith, being much more precious*
*than of gold that perisheth, though it be tried with fire,*
*might be found unto praise and honour and glory at*
*the appearing of Jesus Christ.*

—1 Peter 1:7

Trials by fire are what test our sincerity. Going through difficult times and stressful situations tests our character. If we have any dishonesty or lack sincerity, it will be revealed to us by these "fiery" events.

When you say the word "insincere" slowly, you can almost hear the hissing of a viper. A lack of sincerity is like a poisonous snake that lurks in the background, unnoticed until it suddenly strikes, oozing forth its harmful venom.

## Getting the Wax Out

As wax made the vessel look good, by covering up imperfections rather than exposing and eliminating them, so we often use the wax of insincerity to cover up many of our emotional blemishes. As fire melted the wax and revealed what was really there, so trials can have a similar effect in our lives. When everything is going well, when there is no pressure or heat, everything looks good. When the adversities of life bring trouble, our true character is revealed.

Like the melting of the wax, fire reveals the true condition of our heart. We think the things we go through in life—the struggles with children, financial problems, or marital problems—are there to harm us, but the truth is, if we have a mature attitude toward life, we understand that really these things are often the fire of God to show us our character defects.

Our thoughts and how we speak help us deal with these defects, and if we are honest enough to hear and to speak honestly in love, they help us as well as others. The key is to deal with ourselves and others in love. Words, even if they are true, will never bring forth beneficial lasting change unless they are rooted in love.

"The Prayer of Love" gives you the power to be genuine. We can be sincere, honest in our relationships with others and our understanding of ourselves. We are not pressured to be something other than what we are, but we are confident and at peace because we understand who we are and what we are destined to do in God's purpose.

In our modern world it is hard to find sincere people. To be sincere, one must be genuine and willing to speak truthfully from the heart. The risks involved in such honesty make sincerity a very precious commodity. It is impossible for a person to be sincere without the pursuit for honesty. Sincerity must be rooted in love, and based upon spiritual knowledge and discernment. It must be demonstrated by the approving of excellence. Only then can true sincerity reveal itself.

Hypocrisy is the opposite of sincerity. Hypocrisy tries to make that which is artificial seem real. It is not genuine, and its source is in fear, not love. As we go through the benchmarks from love to knowledge to discernment to excellence, we find that the funnel becomes increasingly narrower. This is because the last three benchmarks that allow us to measure spiritual maturity—sincerity, offense, and righteousness—are continual stumbling blocks to honest, open, and loving relationships.

All loving relationships that develop and are lasting require sincerity. People often "fall in love," but the point at which we progress from infatuation to fondness to affection and into true love is marked by a willingness and openness to seek genuine sincerity. If people cannot be honest with themselves, they will never be honest with anyone else.

However, genuine sincerity that is rooted in honesty requires us to allow love, knowledge, discernment, and excellence to mold within us a character capable and willing to endure the opposition and unpleasantness that often accompany being truly sincere.

Genuine sincerity at times causes separation. Anyone can tell another what that person wants to hear. It is easy to be deceptively complimentary—"You're right; you're the best; it was not your fault; no one could have done more"— but it is quite another to love enough to be honest, discreet, and forthright at all times with all people.

The Scriptures tells us to "Let your yes be simply yes and your no be simply no; anything more than that comes from the evil one" (Matthew 5:37, The Amplified Bible). We should try in everything we do to make our yes be simply yes, and our no be simply no. In other words, say what we mean, and

*It's not so much what you think but how you think that determines your character.*

mean what we say, and be willing to stand by our words. To do this with others can be dangerous. Not everyone will accept our words or our beliefs. To do this with ourselves is impossible, unless we have love through the benchmarks active in our life.

How many people do you know who, if asked, "Are you

sincere?" would answer, "No, I'm not." Most people generally believe that they are, but without the establishment of proper benchmarks, there is no way of really knowing, for there is no way to accurately measure your maturity.

## SINCERITY TRAPS

One of the words for offense in the Bible is the Greek word "*skandalon*," which is related to the Latin word "*scandalum*," from which we get our English word "scandal." In addition to offense, the Greek and Latin roots suggest a stumbling block, trap, or snare. Offense is a trap. Like a snare waiting to catch unsuspecting prey, people who are offended become trapped by their own offense. Scandals are actions or events that cause disgrace, outrage, and dishonor and that are rooted in a lack of sincerity.

We all fall into traps. Perhaps the worst trap is found in thinking and speaking wrongly. We are trapped by our words. Words are living things, and thoughts are simply words held captive in the mind that, if released, create an aroma or a stench in whatever atmosphere they are released and can never be taken back. They are living, and once they become spoken, they manifest into the material world.

In the opening verses of the Book of Genesis, God did not think the world into existence; He spoke, "Let there be light: and there was light." There was no light when He thought; there was light when He spoke. That's why, by the words of our mouth, we are either condemned or justified.

So to be sincere is to say what we mean, and mean what we say. The happiest people in the world are those who don't have to go back and try to remember what their lies were. They don't have to keep a file on what they say to assist them with remembering what they said or to whom they said it. Sincerity brings with it the great reward of peace.

## "THE PRAYER OF LOVE"
## EMPHASIZING SINCERITY

*And this I pray, that your love may abound yet more and more in knowledge and in all judgment; That ye may approve things that are excellent; <u>that ye may be sincere</u> and without offense till the day of Christ; Being filled with the fruits of righteousness, which are by Jesus Christ, unto the glory and praise of God.*

# Point of Love

*Being faithful in the little things is, in many ways, the sincerest act of love. For with "little" acts of love there is usually no grand recognition, no parade or marching band to herald your discharge of duty; this is only the constant and repeated internal impulses of love that manifest themselves in an overwhelming sense of contentment and fulfillment.*

# 7

## DON'T FENCE ME IN

*Without Offense*

In this sixth benchmark of "The Prayer of Love," you will learn to pray "let me be without offense." If we don't really care about other people, then there is no reason to gauge or to develop maturity. Why should I want to tell the truth? Why should I have concern for others? Why should I take responsibility? The only reason is because I desire and choose to love.

I desire to live in an atmosphere of love that produces peace and positive interaction with others, rather than in an atmosphere of control where my wants and needs become my overriding pursuit.

We all gravitate toward people who demonstrate compassion and genuine concern, and we tend to avoid those who are self-serving and self-absorbed. Loving actions or attitudes contrary to love don't just happen, but are a result of character. A mature person will respond in love in all situations because love is a result of their growth in maturity and is not easily altered by circumstances.

The immature person will respond to difficult situations by using accusation or intimidation or manipulation to protect their position. They create an atmosphere around themselves that hinders the ability of others to enter into meaningful relationships with them. Again, the benchmarks of "The Prayer of Love" build upon one another. That sequence must start with love and filter down. Sincerity must be an attribute before we can deal with offense. Offense is a great killer, and it is the place where most people are stuck.

## COMEUPPANCE

When I was a young minister, God had greatly blessed my efforts so that the lives of many were dramatically changed as I preached across the nation. By my early twenties, I had gained a reputation among pastors, in certain ministry circles, that I was the one to invite into their church if they wanted to "see things happen."

The truth is that many signs and wonders had followed my ministry, and this made people excited and eager to see me. This was not due to any power of my own, but solely because God, for His purpose, had graced my ministry.

At that time I had a very dear friend who was also a pastor. He was much older and more experienced in ministry than I, so he became for me a sort of mentor. I often sought his help and counsel. So when I started hearing persistent rumors about my ministry that were untrue, and doors for preaching began to close, and the source of this gossip was traced back to my friend, I was baffled.

When I tried calling him to find out what was going on, he refused to take my calls.

He lived in a town several hundred miles away. One day I got in my car and decided to drive to his town to discuss the matter. During the long trip to his office, I searched my heart, but couldn't think of anything I might have done or said that would have made him behave in such a manner. When I arrived, he met me at the door. I asked why he wouldn't return my calls and if he had been the one spreading this gossip.

With a smirk on his face, he acknowledged that he had. I asked him why he was spreading these untrue rumors. Was there something I had done? Had I offended him in some way? "If so," I said, "please forgive me!"

He looked me in the face, and said, "Boy, it's about time you got your comeuppance"—a southern way of saying, it's about time you got what you deserved. With that, he laughed and closed the door in my face.

On the way home, I wept. Within me was a growing desire to reject him and to speak evil of him. I felt bitterness growing within me, due to his rejection and the way he had wronged me. But then an amazing thing happened. God showed me His love. I was reminded of mistakes I had made in my life and things for which He had forgiven me. I began to see that the same spirit that was controlling my friend would control me if I didn't choose love over retaliation.

I would later come to see that on that day God taught

me one part of "The Prayer of Love" that allowed me to love even my enemies. From that day forward, I carried no resentment for this man, but only a desire to love.

## CREATING AN ATMOSPHERE OF FORGIVENESS

God is greater than the opposition that comes against you. Your victory is not dependent on someone else, but is as close as your willingness to choose love. Be advised that peace and joy do not proceed but follow your decision to love, and that decision may involve a process of time.

Like the air we breathe, our love—or lack of love—creates a spiritual atmosphere surrounding us. If our atmosphere is composed primarily of love, then it gives life to us and all around us. If, however, what we produce is rooted in a lack of forgiveness and anger, then the atmosphere we produce becomes toxic to life.

Forgiveness is a mighty force in love. Forgiveness has the power to transform your attitudes and actions from fear to love. Forgiveness restores our relationships with each other and with God. When forgiving, you release yourself and potentially the one you forgive from the bondage of fear.

Contained within the word "forgive" is a description of its purpose. It is for giving. As rejection is the method for enforcing fear, forgiving is literally the method for-giving or restoring love.

Forgiveness is an act of restoration back into a loving state. Those who forgive are making a conscious choice to love. When you choose not to forgive, the one you hurt the most is yourself. It is a form of self-punishment. And though most people think they are punishing the one they are angry with, they are really being controlled by events and attitudes.

The solution to offense is forgiveness. When we are offended, we always show disrespect to the source of the offense. We feel wronged and therefore the last thing we are going to give that person or thing that caused this wrong is our forgiveness.

The whole world is offended. People are hurt. The issue is how to "get over it," but how can we get over it? We need help. The antidote to being offended is forgiveness, but forgiveness is not merely the mouthing of words such as "I forgive you," or "Will you forgive me?" Forgiveness can only come from within our spirit.

Offense is at the narrowest part of the funnel. This can be the most difficult thing to overcome when striving to love. When we are wronged, we feel we have a right to reject others and lash out.

We will never effectively deal with any issue of offense before we first decide that we want to follow after love in that situation. We can have no release from the crippling effects of our offense before we choose to seek love. This is why people can be offended over seemingly insignificant things and can let that offense continue for years, even to the grave.

But offense has become a graveyard for the dreams of many. An inability to progress toward a goal and the debilitating effects of depression can often be traced to offense. We must learn to forgive.

Forgiveness is the key to our mental and emotional prisons. Whether our offense is the result of our own actions or those of others, the result is the same. Offense is a crippler even if the cause of the offense is 100 percent the fault of another person. We need to embrace forgiveness, if we are to be set free.

We might feel justified in being offended, but it will never provide mental or emotional liberty. The word "forgive" contains the solution within its structure. For-give-ness is the ability to give forth.

Only forgiveness has the ability to negate every evil and harmful act. It is a learned art that is fully practiced by only a few who have witnessed its power to unleash love.

Corrie ten Boom, the Christian holocaust survivor, helped many Jews escape the Nazis during World War II. She, along with her sister, Betsie, eventually wound up in a concentration camp for their activities. Years later she relayed this illustration of the power of forgiveness:

The guard over their area of the camp was a vindictive and brutal man who had beaten many unmercifully and even contributed to Betsie's death. After the war, Corrie wrote a book, *The Hiding Place*, then traveled around telling people of those difficult days and God's goodness in the harshest of times.

While giving a speech on God's goodness and the power of forgiveness, the former concentration camp guard was in the audience and desired the forgiveness she spoke about. He came before her and asked for her forgiveness not even recognizing who she was or the hardship he had caused her personally. He only knew that she was a prisoner in the camp and he wanted her forgiveness.

*The highest fences any of us ever build are fences of doubt, hurt, pride, and suspicion.*

It was a great test for Corrie. Would she forgive this man face to face who had caused such pain to others, including her sister? This man wanted more of the God of love that she spoke of, but how difficult it was to give him the forgiveness he sought. This prison guard as well as Corrie's spiritual maturity were being tested. Would she demonstrate the greatest of love through her forgiveness, or would her feeling of offense at this man cause prison walls of her own making, to keep her from progressing in love and maturity?

She did forgive this man, which not only opened up access for him to God's greater love but also caused the power of God's love to be multiplied in her.

Spiritually mature people will recognize that when they are being challenged to forgive another, God is judging their maturity. Think of being cut off by someone in traffic or having a neighbor behave in a not-so-neighborly manner. Who among us has not had others speak unpleasant and hurtful things to us? Who has not known, at some time, the rejection of someone close to them? And who has not lashed out at some imagined or real wrong caused by the government, a business, a family member, a friend, a teacher, or a coworker?

Such instances are common, but do we realize that they are opportunities for our spiritual maturity? Our maturity is tested by the severity of the offense. If we do not learn to forgive in little things, we will never forgive in great things.

*Harboring offense causes you to suffer for someone else's wrong.*

Forgiveness needs to be practiced if its power is to grow, yet how many fail to practice it even in small things? To the person who lacks spiritual maturity, forgiveness is a weakness, but to those seeking it, it is the power to tear down strongholds and release prisoners.

Anger and bitterness are the children of offense. When we choose not to forgive for any reason, we allow a seed of bitterness to take root, and that root of bitterness will eventually kill the one who refuses to forgive. The world often equates forgiveness to weakness, but the truth is, it takes great strength to forgive.

Forgiving someone for a wrong they've done does not necessarily mean that there are no consequences for their wrong action. I can forgive someone for meaning me harm and burning down my house, but that does not mean that that person will not be arrested or have to pay compensation or pay in some other fashion for their crime. Though they will face consequences, my forgiving them sets me free from the evil that was directed at me and allows them an opportunity to be delivered from it as well.

If you look at offense as a spirit that is living and attaches itself to anyone who accepts it, then we see behind the act of offense. The Book of Hebrews 12:15 warns us to look "diligently lest any root of bitterness springing up trouble you, and thereby many be defiled."

In the biblical story of Esau and Jacob, we have a perfect illustration of this. Isaac had twin sons, Esau and Jacob—Esau being the slightly older and the favorite of his father had the birthright to the inheritance. Esau, however, cared little for spiritual things and sold his birthright to Jacob. Jacob was not totally honorable, but tricked his blind father into giving him his blessing as well.

When Esau found out what was done, he set out to kill Jacob. Even though he had freely sold his birthright to Jacob, he felt wronged. Though they made amends with each other, Esau harbored a root of bitterness.

Esau was the father of the Edomites, and today the descendants of Esau and Jacob are still at war with one another in the Middle East, more than three thousand years later.

Jesus, in his parable about the servant who was forgiven by his master but would not forgive the one who owed him, told of how his master delivered him to the tormentors until all that was due was paid. Jesus said, "So shall my heavenly Father also do to each of you who from the heart will not forgive his brother his trespasses."

The main point is not that God is going to punish us if we don't forgive, but rather that in not forgiving we punish ourselves and are tormented by anger and bitterness. Only forgiveness from the heart can release us from this torment.

Offense is a trap. Have you ever loaned someone some money, and they did not give it back? A little while later you saw them with a fancy coat or a shiny wristwatch or a new car. You got angry and thought to yourself, "They have money to buy these things and can't even pay me back." You may cuss the daylights out of them, kick the cat, and slam the door because you're so angry. You are the one who is trapped. They may be enjoying their new purchase, but you are controlled by your feeling of offense.

## THE BLACKJACK TREE IN YOUR LIFE

It is like the story of the man who planted an orange grove. He planted a whole grove of new orange trees, and he waited for years for them to mature. He painstakingly tended the orchard, pulling off the blossoms one by one from the trees in this beautiful little orchard so they would bear more fruit.

He did this for three years; in the fourth year, he let the fruit grow, and he had the most beautiful pieces of fruit, but when he came to eat them, they were very bitter. He couldn't understand it. He had a fence around the whole orchard; he had cultivated it, kept it clean, used only the finest trees, yet the fruit was bitter.

So he went around and around and still couldn't figure it out. Finally way down at the far corner on the other side of the fence he found a blackjack tree. The old farmers say that the blackjack tree not only takes nectar into the root system from the soil but it also gives off a terrible bitterness from the roots.

The roots of that blackjack tree had grown under the fence and had wrapped around those of the fruit trees. The fruit was bitter because of one blackjack tree outside of the fence down in the far corner of the orchard.

That blackjack tree is like offense that we allow. It builds up a root of bitterness that injures our good fruit. Our peace, our joy, our hopes and dreams—they all become contaminated if we don't deal with the offense.

This is reminiscent of what the prophet said: yet I plant

of thee a holy, noble vine, how did it get turned into a degenerate plant?

## EQUAL OPPORTUNITY OFFENSE

Almost everyone is hurting from something, and sometimes it is God whom we blame. Why did God let this happen? How could God let three thousand people die in the World Trade Center (which some Muslims say was an answer to their prayer)? Or let a tsunami kill tens of thousands (which some Christians say was God's judgment because it happened in a predominantly Muslim part of the world)? Offense cuts across all religious, social, and ethnic lines.

The truth is, we live in a world whose natural actions have spiritual consequences. There is a certain wobble in the spirit world just like there is in the spinning and rotation of the earth so that every so many years, we have a leap year. Like the leap year, every so often there should come in our lives a time that we make an adjustment—a time to judge our spiritual maturity. Maybe at those times we should go back and take a closer look at our life and see why things are not working the way we think they should work.

Offense becomes a wild organism that clogs the sea of our life, shuts off the harbors of our life, and stops the transport of our life. If we allow that organism to work, it will affect our view of all things.

When we are sincere and we don't harbor offense, then love through knowledge, discernment, and excellence will bring to us the fruits of righteousness. When I pray "let me be without offense," I empower God to release me and to restore in me the full fruit of His salvation.

## "THE PRAYER OF LOVE" EMPHASIZING OFFENSE

*And this I pray, that your love may abound yet more and more in knowledge and in all judgment; That ye may approve things that are excellent; that ye may be sincere and <u>without offense</u> till the day of Christ; Being filled with the fruits of righteousness, which are by Jesus Christ, unto the glory and praise of God.*

# POINT OF LOVE

*We have all built fences to protect us
from pain and hurt.*

*If we can't find the grace to tear down these fences
all at once, may we at least learn
how to open gates to the potential of
life-altering love.*

# 8

## FRUIT IS ALWAYS FOUND OUT ON A LIMB

*Becoming Filled with Fruit*

We are each of us angels with only one wing; and we can only
fly by embracing one another.

—LUCIANO DE CRESCENZO

## LEARNING TO FLY TOGETHER

World War II had just concluded. Japan had surrendered,
but on a far outpost in New Guinea, an American soldier
and a Japanese officer were engaged in a severe life-and-
death struggle, neither knowing that the war had ended.

The American soldier had become separated from his squad two weeks earlier and had run into the jungle, pursued by the Japanese. These Japanese soldiers had become isolated and abandoned on the island of New Guinea when major fighting ceased and the brunt of the war moved on to other Pacific islands.

While foraging for food early one morning along the jungle pathway, a command was yelled out in clear English with a Japanese accent, "GI, put your hands up and surrender." The soldier instinctively chose to run instead of surrender, and as he did, shots rang out in his direction as he sought his escape.

Running down a steep embankment, he stepped on a booby trap, which was composed of several razor-sharp bamboo pikes that lacerated his leg, which bled profusely. He bandaged his leg the best he could and realized that, because of the condition of his leg, his only hope for survival was to surrender.

Strangely, he was not being pursued. He painstakingly made his way back onto the path and toward the place where he had been ordered to surrender. Upon hearing movement ahead, he slowly crept up and found a Japanese officer by himself. As he peered through the undergrowth, he could see that the officer's head was bandaged and thus he could not see beyond a couple of feet due to a grenade flash that had damaged his eyesight.

After observing the Japanese officer for a long while, the soldier made known his presence. Thus began a back-and-forth conversation, both wanting the other to lay down their arms, neither willing to surrender. After a time they realized that unless they worked together, neither was likely to escape the jungle alive. They agreed on a temporary truce.

So began their bizarre journey out of the jungle: The Japanese officer, carrying the brunt of the soldier's weight, and the soldier, being the eyes for the officer. The officer was educated before the war at the University of California, and the soldier himself was from California, and on that common ground, they found camaraderie. They had little to do but walk and talk, and slowly an uneasy friendship, birthed out of each other's desperate need, began to grow.

*Being righteous is its own reward.*

The unspoken thought of each concerned what they would do with the other once their rescue drew near. Would the officer wrestle away the soldier's rifle and kill the soldier, or would the soldier try to slay the officer?

When they finally made it to a place where patrols were likely to pick them up, neither chose hostility toward the other. The companionship of adversity gave them a mutual respect, though they each had opportunity to destroy the other. Their mutual experience gave them power over their offense and created a situation in which they, in sincerity, desired life for the other.

## The Limb of Love
## Never Breaks No Matter
## How Far Out You Climb

Like these soldiers, we each have instances in life where we can choose to let the strengths of another overcome our weaknesses. Our willingness to connect in our need allows us to fly together on the wings of love. People who develop abundant spiritual fruit are never afraid of going out on a limb to love others.

The act of becoming is the process of spiritual maturity in our lives. We become what we behold, and if we are able to behold the nature of God in an ever-clearer manner, we will become what He is—love, compassion, justice, joy, truth, honor, peace—the image of the invisible God.

I have two pear trees in my backyard that were planted at the same time. Each year they both have pears, but where one brings only a handful of fruit each year, the other provides so much fruit that I have an abundance and give most of it to others.

A tree can have some fruit without being filled with fruit. Likewise, we can have spiritual fruit without being filled with fruit. I may be a person who has some concern for my fellow man, some love, some compassion, some desire for spiritual things, some passion to find and fulfill my purpose, but I may not be filled with these things.

Being filled with the fruit of righteousness means I have the ability to possess the fruit beyond measure. There is joy but there is also full joy. There is peace, but there is also perfect peace. There is love, but there is also unconditional love. Each attribute of spiritual maturity has a perfection that we can attain. We can become filled with the fruit of righteousness.

How we tend what is given to us by God will determine the quality and quantity of our fruit. Becoming fruitful is not so much about the fruit as it is about our ability to produce fruit. Spiritual maturity gives us that ability.

If I am going to become full of fruit, then I must not only think right, I must also be right. We are told to seek first the Kingdom of God and His righteousness—literally His ways of being and doing. In other words, who is God and how does He act? You've heard the statement "There's a right way and a wrong way to do everything." The right way, as it pertains to our discussion, is the God way or the spiritual way. The wrong way is the carnal way—that which does not originate in the spirit, but in our fleshly thoughts and desires.

## THE POSSIBILITY OF RIGHTEOUSNESS PRODUCES HOPE

We need to encourage one another, but we also need to challenge one another. We can become better. We are not failures without the possibility of improvement. We each are valuable instruments for the demonstration of love. Many may live below their destiny, but it does not have to be that way. Love has the power to deliver.

I was delivering a message on righteousness in a conference in West Virginia about a dozen years ago. I was speaking about how we can all change: there are no lost causes. I relayed to those gathered that change begins with a decision, and that the consequence of right decisions will produce righteous fruit.

Afterward a man from the audience (who has since become well known and influential) stood in line a long time to speak with me. He drew me aside and said, "Sir, I am a failure, I've lost everything, but today I have hope." This man had been having an extramarital affair for many years. His wife was divorcing him, his finances were in ruins, and he was losing his family.

Why did he have hope? Because, for whatever reason, that night he understood that love was stronger than his weakness, and love was stronger than his failure. His hope was that he could not only change but also become righteous, and God's righteousness would produce fruit in his life.

From that night, he dramatically and completely changed. In a great miracle of events, he was restored with his wife and family. Instead of living for himself, he put his life into other people. Today his influence has been felt throughout the world, and thousands of men and women look to him for counsel and spiritual direction.

Righteousness exalts a person, a family, or a nation.

This individual was exalted before others and is now highly acclaimed because he believed that righteousness was possible.

# Righteousness Is the Spiritual Way

Righteousness is the art of being right and acting right, which comes from acquiring God's righteousness—His right ways of thinking and acting. Righteousness is simply being and doing what is right. If I find someone's wallet, and it has $800 in it and it also has a driver's license and identification in it, I have to make a decision as to what is right. If I have spiritual maturity, I do what's right and return the wallet, but without spiritual maturity, what is right and wrong may become blurred.

I may say to myself, "How fortunate that I found this money since I have such a need," or I may recognize the owner as someone who is well off and say to myself, "I need this far more than he does." I rationalize my behavior, because I lack righteousness.

Years ago you didn't have to worry much about people

doing what was right because people would give you their word, often doing business on a handshake. There have always been cons and crooks, but for the most part, you could pretty much take your neighbor's word because society operated, more or less, on the principle of the Ten Commandments and the Golden Rule. A person's reputation meant something to them because they respected the opinion of their friends and neighbors and had shame. If they failed in keeping their word, they would be, in one degree or another, embarrassed or ashamed of their conduct.

Today, however, there is no shame because traditional standards have broken down, and love is growing cold. Many professional athletes and movie stars openly speak of their sexual exploits. One even claimed that he had slept with more than a thousand women and fathered an unknown number of children. Corporations like Enron lie bald-faced to the public and dupe private shareholders out of billions. And frauds like Bernie Madoff bilk investors out of billions of dollars. Little, if any, remorse—except for the sorrow of being caught—is ever shown.

*Becoming righteous starts with learning God's value system and adopting it as your own.*

The politically correct efforts to foster self-esteem and negate personal responsibility have unfortunately worked all too well. Truth is now far too often in the eye of the beholder. We no longer have a societal consciousness of right and wrong or a social standard about what is appropriate conduct, and, as a society, we are becoming increasingly spiritually immature. Guilt, regret, and shame for doing wrong should be emotional responses to spiritually immature actions. They are like circuit breakers that interrupt a mechanical process when it is not operating properly.

When we are not operating in maturity, these spiritual circuit breakers should short-circuit our wrong attitudes and actions. They are part of our conscience, and a well-developed conscience is itself a fruit of spiritual maturity.

## Finding What Was Lost

Too many people have lost a sense of righteousness. The way to get it back is one person at a time, and we each need to be the first person to submit our will to make a conscious and determined effort to think, do, say, and become righteous—to have a willingness to say, "I'm going to do better; in fact, I'm going to do my best." It first starts out as a love for others and respect for your God-given potential.

These benchmarks, working in order—love, knowledge, judgment, excellence, sincerity, and not being offended—and working from a godly perspective rather than out of emotions, will automatically cause me to want to do the right thing. That is the result of allowing these benchmarks to cause me to mature spiritually. If I am having a struggle with doing the right thing, I can go back through each benchmark and examine myself. The fact that it is a fruit means that it's not just doing the right thing, but that, in my choice, it becomes instinctive.

Righteousness becomes a quality of who I am, not just what I do. I begin reaping the benefit of having this spiritual order in my life. I become whole. I have integrity or wholeness in my life because these spiritual benchmarks cause me to enhance a godly character. It is right to have love; it is right to have knowledge; it is right to have judgment; it's right to have vision or excellence; it is right to be sincere; it is right to be without offense, and consequently, I reap the fruit of that righteousness.

Righteousness (the way God thinks and acts) exalts a

nation, but sin brings reproach. As we are filled with the fruits of righteousness, thinking and acting as God does, we appropriate His victory over sin. Our life is no longer centered on avoiding or dealing with sin, but on living as an overcoming vessel of God in His plan. We become transformed by "The Prayer of Love" into the image of God, taking on His nature.

## "The Prayer of Love" Focusing on Bringing Forth Divine Fruit

*And this I pray, that your love may abound yet more and more in knowledge and in all judgment; That ye may approve things that are excellent; that ye may be sincere and without offense till the day of Christ; Being filled with the fruits of righteousness, which are by Jesus Christ, unto the glory and praise of God.*

# POINT OF LOVE

------

*A person who has love can never be a failure and a person with great wealth and ability without love can never really be considered a success.*

*Peace, patience, faithfulness, kindness, goodness, gentleness, truth, hope, fulfillment, faith, sacrifice, and discipline are all fruit that grow on the tree of love.*

# 9

## NEVER-ENDING LOVE

*Love is not a euphoric emotion; it is an act of the will surrounded by emotions.*

—MARK HANBY

## LOCKED IN LOVE'S EMBRACE

When I lived in Fort Worth, I had a small fishing boat that I kept at the Rocky Creek Marina on Benbrook Lake. One afternoon I drove out to the lake to do some fishing and as I approached the boat landing, I noticed a large commotion going on down by the water.

Rescue vehicles had been called, and they were searching the lake for a man and his son who had been feared drowned. That part of the lake had a steep drop-off. Earlier, a group of people had been picnicking, and their four-year-old boy had wandered away and fallen into the water. His father had apparently seen him from a distance and had run to save his son. The father did not know how to swim, but his paternal love for his young son had caused him to dive in after him, if by some chance he would be able to save him.

I can still remember the sight as they dredged the bodies up from the bottom of the lake. As they pulled them out of the water, the father had his arms wrapped tightly around the son. It was such a great tragedy for the family, and yet such an example of supreme love—a father unwilling to let go of his son even at the point of death.

Today we can make a conscious decision to love. Love is in our possession, and we have the power to give it to everyone with whom we come in contact. We cannot control whether or not they are willing to receive it, but we can always give love.

# GROWING IN MATURITY
## NEVER ENDS

We may never come to the place where we find out all there is to know about the benchmarks of "The Prayer of Love." As you continue in your desire to find and grow in love, these benchmarks become a continual practice in your life.

There comes a point as we mature that we begin to understand that eternal truths are infinite truths, that is, they are not limited to time or dimension, and they have no end. So the love is infinite in its power to transform us. We do not come to the place where we stop growing in love. Though this prayer will bring us to perfection or maturity, the infinite wonder and love that is God will continue to manifest in us and through us without end.

"The Prayer of Love" will bring you to the place where love continually overrules your carnal nature, and at that point, you are really at the beginning of a marvelous spiritual journey. There is no end to love, so we are going to realize that the ways of God are past "finding out," that is, God is infinite so love can grow eternally.

You can find, but you can't find out. You can dig into

the barrel, but you can't reach the bottom because it has an infinite source that is continually filling it with increased love and more knowledge and greater possibility. As the prophet said more than twenty-five hundred years ago, the ways and thoughts of God are greater than the ways and thoughts of man. It is plugging into this source through maturity and love that unlocks your divine potential.

## HUMAN LOVE TO SUPERNATURAL LOVE

The benchmarks of "The Prayer of Love" provide a comparison between human love and human ability and supernatural love and supernatural ability. There is natural ability and supernatural ability. There is a natural love and a supernatural love. There is knowledge and there is a supernatural knowledge. There is judgment and there is supernatural judgment. "The Prayer of Love" asks God to affect the supernatural in us.

If you allow this pattern of the funnel—starting with love and going through to the fruits of righteousness—to become a continual pattern in your life, it will, by itself, change you. Love is like that. It has a power all by itself to accomplish its will.

You should not think of this pattern as "to do" steps for changing your life. It is not about your efforts, but God's love and power to help you change and mature. What is required from you, the reader, is desire—desire to find, accept, give, and grow in love.

It is only in recognizing and embracing our identity in Christ that we have the means to overcome our carnal nature. The benchmarks are spiritual portals that allow us to go through one spiritual door after another. "The Prayer of Love" is the power to manifest the character of God through your distinctive personality. You are the vessel of God for His righteousness. You are a light that cannot be hidden. In praying "The Prayer of Love," you partake of and become the love that is God.

## LOVE WILL BREAK OUT

Great love usually manifests itself in great struggle and sacrifice. One of the reasons deep love is so prevalent at many funerals is that the loss shocks those gathered into the reality of love for that person, their family, and their friends. They will no longer see each other in this earthly existence, and what has been lost and the possibility of what could have been must be dealt with in a few short, passing hours. Our sorrow in many ways becomes a measure of the love that was experienced or was desired.

Love is always manifesting itself in the smallest acts of kindness and in the great occurrences of sacrifice. From time to time, it reveals itself on a massive scale that even the spiritually blind cannot ignore. Love, on a wide scale, has broken out at different times throughout history.

The Kingdom of God will come when love rules the earth. When we choose to love, we work toward that day and toward the manifestation of God who is love. Though there are many examples of love breaking out, none to this point has maintained a momentum that would deliver all humankind from its ordeal.

India, prior to independence from the British, was a country with two large religious groups composed of Muslims and Hindus. After independence, warfare broke out between these two groups. Mahatma Gandhi, a respected spiritual leader of the country, went on a hunger strike that was instrumental in quelling the violence. This came about not by the will or efforts of men, but by the force of love. One man had a willingness to lose all to gain peace, and it transformed the situation. Although peace did not last, it demonstrated the power of love to defuse even highly volatile situations.

In the Christmas truce of 1915, love manifested in a miraculous way as well. The Allies and the Germans had been fighting and dying in unbelievable hardship by the tens of thousands. So great was the carnage that on the Somme battlefield alone, more than a million soldiers lay dead by the end of the war.

On Christmas Eve, across various parts of the line, Allied and German soldiers began to sing "Silent Night" and other Christmas songs, each in their own language. Soon, they rose from the trenches to meet in no-man's-land and exchange candy and cigarettes and share stories. Men by the thousands, who had only hours earlier been killing one another, acted like comrades.

This did not happen in every place, but in many places over several days. They had become so friendly that some even played games of football. The hardship and sacrifices of war had put within their spirit a desire for peace and this outbreak of a manifestation of love.

Commanders on both sides became so fearful of this

fraternization that they forbade any contact with the opposing forces. When this did not work, some even resorted to shelling their own soldiers in an effort to get them back into the war. The opportunity for love eventually succumbed to fear, however, and the war resumed.

This has also happened during the American Civil War and other conflicts. At Fredericksburg, for example, in the evening, Union and Confederate soldiers would meet down by the creek to exchange tobacco and food and to share the fellowship of suffering soldiers.

The unmasking of the true inner spirit is continually seen in lives willing to love. As with those above, we all have the possibility of greater loving response by yielding our human resistance. Tragedy often lowers our spiritual yielding point to where we are willing to entertain what otherwise our fears would limit.

## WHAT YOU ARE TO BECOME

Take courage; though love at times seems elusive and difficult to find, it cannot be stopped in those who are willing to yield to its influence. It is a very personal possession that no one can take from you or force you to give or receive. You must be willing to yield what you are for what you are to become. The world likewise must be willing to yield its suspicions, arrogance, disobedience, and fear in order to become a world ruled by love. "The Prayer of Love" provides you with this pattern. Your willingness to embrace each aspect of the prayer will cause love to abound in your life. People who choose to love, regardless of their imperfections, become a light to the world. Your love is a great light to your world.

Love is not a rest stop along life's journey or something to be obtained so we can go on to other things. Love is the ultimate goal of all life. Love will become our lifestyle as we allow it to mature us and change us into its image.

In speaking of troubled times, Jesus said the following words: "And because iniquity shall abound, the love of many shall wax cold. But he that shall endure unto the end, the same shall be saved. And this gospel of the kingdom shall be preached in all the world for a witness unto all nations; and then shall the end come" (Matthew 24:12–14).

I believe this portion of scripture is often misunderstood and unfortunately is frequently used to engender fear in the reader rather than to bring direction. Since fear is the opposite of love, anything that you allow to produce fear within you will diminish your ability to love. When lawlessness and evil abound, the love of many will grow cold, but this does not have to be the case in your life, nor should it be.

Jesus said, "You are the light of the world" (Matthew 5:14, The Amplified Bible)—that light emanates from your love. Many people today are fearful of an uncertain world economy and evil that manifests itself in a variety of ways. They no longer feel safe in their communities or secure in their future. In the above passage, Jesus is telling us not to let the iniquity of the world affect our love; instead, we need to endure in our love and let it grow and shine to the end. The gospel (good news) of the Kingdom of God is based on the fact that His love has triumphed and so will your love.

How will current events in the world be resolved? Some foresee them being decided by warfare and bloodshed and an army led by Jesus forcefully and violently destroying rulers and opposing nations and imposing His will upon the world. That we live in troubling times is apparent to most, but I sense in my spirit that the reformation of the world into a kingdom of peace will not come through force and physical violence on the part of God or those seeking to follow God, but through the power and force of God's love revealed in and through them.

Love is the most powerful force in the universe; however, most people do not realize this one glorious and supreme truth: to find love is to find God. When you become awakened by the reality and power of His love, all fear will leave you; when the world becomes awakened to His love, fear and discord will leave it as well. You can become an instrument to bring forth a kingdom of peace not by wielding a physical weapon or by intimidating and coercing those opposed to you, but by using the sword of His truth in love. Those who love are the hope of the world.

For thousands of years people have sought to resolve their differences and live in harmony by establishing various forms of government, developing benevolent social organizations, and passing laws, but also through utilizing threats, manipulation, violence, and warfare. Though people from time to time have been able to fashion societies with a semblance of order and freedom, man has yet to bring about the sought-after utopia of a kingdom of perfect abundance, security, and peace.

This, I believe, will change in our day. Love will find

a way to dislodge the inhumanity and fear of the world and steadily water our hopes and dreams with its wonder and power. Since love cannot be forced upon anyone, for the world to change and find love it must do so freely and willingly. The events in the world today are a catalyst to foster this change, so don't become afraid of the future but rather embrace it for the opportunities it offers you to grow in and to demonstrate love. People increasingly desire a way to be freed from their fears. Where every other device has failed, love will transform the world.

"The Prayer of Love" is the way to ask for God's transformational power. Love is the vehicle and "The Prayer of Love" can become the pattern to end the immaturity of humankind and bring forth universal peace.

It will happen.

Death will be swallowed up by life.

Love will rule the earth.

Though you can influence others, you cannot make love happen for them, but you possess the power to allow it to happen within yourself. And if you allow it to happen within yourself, it will become a seed that is able to grow and flourish until your life and all around you are influenced by its fragrance. Allow "The Prayer of Love" to be a vehicle to bring forth your spiritual maturity as you become transformed by love.

When you choose love, you become God's answer. You take on the important mission of changing your world for good. This book contains many fascinating and powerful insights on love. No doubt the concepts within this book have already stimulated your thoughts and the possibility of acquiring a lifestyle marked by love. The principles contained within this book will not be fully realized by one reading of the text. To further help establish this prayer in your life, we have developed *A Study in the Prayer of Love* and *The Prayer of Love Devotional*, which are also available for your use. They provide daily tools to help with your continual transformation by "The Prayer of Love."

## "THE PRAYER OF LOVE"

*And this I pray, that your love may abound yet more and more in knowledge and in all judgment; That ye may approve things that are excellent; that ye may be sincere and without offense till the day of Christ; Being filled with the fruits of righteousness, which are by Jesus Christ, unto the glory and praise of God.*

Printed in the United States
By Bookmasters